The Stature of Man

ORIGINAL
THE AGE OF DEFEAT

Books by Colin Wilson:
The Outsider
Religion and the Rebel
The Stature of Man

The
Stature
of
Man

BY COLIN WILSON

1959
Houghton Mifflin Company, Boston
The Riverside Press, Cambridge

*The passages from poems by William Butler Yeats
appearing on pages 118, 147 and 154 are quoted from
THE COLLECTED POEMS OF W. B. YEATS and are used
by permission of The Macmillan Company.*

For Eve and Negley
with affection

IT IS perhaps this wrong connection of ideas [that the earth is a mere point in the universe] which has led men to the still falser notion that they are not worthy of the Creator's regard. They have believed themselves to be obeying the dictates of humility when they have denied that the earth and all that the universe contains exists only on man's account, on the ground that the admission of such an idea would be only conceit. But they have not been afraid of the laziness and cowardice which are the inevitable results of this affected modesty. *The present-day avoidance of the belief that we are the highest in the universe is the reason that we have not the courage to work in order to justify that title, that the duties springing from it seem too laborious, and that we would rather abdicate our position and our rights than realize them in all their consequences. Where is the pilot that will guide us between these hidden reefs of conceit and false humility?*

SAINT MARTIN, *quoted from Strindberg's* Legends

Acknowledgments

I wish to acknowledge the help of Negley Farson (who, among other things, first drew my attention to *The Lonely Crowd*), Hugh Heckstall Smith and Bill Hopkins, who offered suggestions for improvement, and Joy Wilson and Dorothy Welford who helped in preparing the manuscript for press. Also to thank Philip Thody, of Belfast University, for suggestions and criticisms on the Sartre chapter.

Contents

Introduction
The Vanishing Hero

The problem that forms the subject of this book first presented itself to me as a question of literature. When I tried to find a phrase that would express it concisely, I hit upon "the unheroic hypothesis." This seemed to define what I was thinking about: the sense of defeat, or disaster, or futility, that seems to underlie so much modern writing. It is not merely that contemporary authors seem to feel bound to deal with the "ordinary man" and his problems; it is that most of them seem incapable of dealing with anything but the most ordinary *states of mind.*

But when I came to consider the reasons for this unheroic premise, I became aware of an attitude of mind that seems to permeate the whole of modern society. I found this more difficult to characterize. As an approximation, I would say that it is a general sense of *insignificance.*

De Tocqueville put his finger on it in *Democracy in America,* when he said of the American: "When he comes to survey the totality of his fellows, and to place himself in contrast to so huge a body, he is instantly overwhelmed by his own insignificance and weakness." And I began to realize that more was in question than a purely literary problem. If the heroes of modern fiction seem negative and defeated, they are only reflecting the world in which their creators live. The first step in understanding the problem of "the vanishing hero" must be an attempt to gain an insight into the "insignificance premise" in modern society. But this in turn needs explaining in terms of the social crises of the twentieth century. Not *entirely* in terms of these crises, of couse; who now accepts the Marxist notion that economics explains everything, even religion? In fact, the problem of the hero provides the ideal refutation of the extreme Marxist position. Social factors can shed an immense amount of light on the subject, but a point comes where there is no alternative but to consider the "metaphysical" problems of the individual. Communism, however sympathetically understood, cannot claim to have solved *all* the problems.

These were the reasons that led me to begin my study of the hero with the evidence of sociology.

Part One

The Evidence
of Sociology

It is the task of history to display the types of compulsion and of violence characteristic of each age.
A. N. WHITEHEAD: *Adventures of Ideas*

It is also my impression that the conditions I believe to be responsible for other-direction are affecting increasing numbers of people in the metropolitan centers of advanced industrial countries. My analysis of the other-directed character is thus at once an analysis of the American and of contemporary man.
DAVID RIESMAN: *The Lonely Crowd*

IN HIS disturbing study of American advertising, *The Hidden Persuaders,* Vance Packard writes: "In 1953, a leading advertising researcher concluded that Americans would have to live a third better if they were to keep pace with growing production and permit the United States economy to hit a $400,000,000,000 gross national product in 1958." It is the phrase "live a third better" that is important here. It means that the American consumer will have to be persuaded to spend a third more money on things he does not really need. It means bigger time-payment schemes, bigger refrigerators and cars and insurance policies. It will follow that he must then make bigger concessions to the need for security, and to the organization that employs him, and must learn to conform more rigorously to its demands for efficiency. In fact, "live a third better" means, in actuality, make the merry-go-round whirl a third faster. Or to use a less festive simile, work the treadmill a third harder.

   J. K. Galbraith has called this "the dependence effect." He sees in it the central fallacy of modern American economics. The fallacy runs like this: "A higher standard of living depends on higher production. Higher production is dependent on higher consumption. Therefore, the best way to improve society is to step up production, and to persuade everyone to consume more." This type of fallacy depends upon taking a premise which is true up to a point, and extending it until it has become false. For instance, it is true that an army fights on its stomach. If an economist then went on to say: "Therefore, we must produce more and more food; and we must all learn to eat more than ever before: in this way we shall become unconquerable," he would be ignoring the fact that over-eating is more likely to produce a nation of ulcerated stomachs than a race of efficient soldiers. *The Hidden Persuaders* makes it apparent that one of the results of persuading Americans to "live a third better" is a kind of moral dyspepsia whose results are quite as harmful as those of widespread poverty.

Vance Packard makes no bones about his reasons for objecting to the "consumer fallacy." He quotes Bernice Allen of Ohio University: "We have no proof that more material goods, such as more cars or gadgets, has made anyone happier." Galbraith is more cautious: "The question of happiness and what adds to it has been evaded." He is only concerned with pointing out that the consumer fallacy is wasteful and inefficient as a social philosophy. "The same week the Russians launched the first earth satellite, we launched a magnificent selection of car models, including the uniquely elegant new Edsel." He suggests that a higher proportion of the national income should be diverted to social uses — schools, parks, research — and that this could easily be done by imposing a higher purchase tax on luxury goods. However, Galbraith's economic theories are outside the range of this essay. What is interesting to note, at this point, is his analysis of the diseases that attack an "affluent society." Galbraith is only one of many American sociologists who feel that something strange and dangerous is happening in America today. And what is happening is only an outcome of the high-powered technical civilization that aims at higher material standards. This form of society is spreading all over the globe; so that, unless a world war calls a halt, there seems no reason why the problems of the affluent society should not reach every country in the world in the course of time.

The problems I wish to touch on in the first part of this essay are not problems of economics, they are problems of the effect upon the individual of increased material security. In 1956 the suicide rate in Sweden was 1 to every 4460 of the population; in Denmark 1 to every 4431. This is more than twice as high as the English rate. These countries are also "affluent societies." Denmark is probably the most highly organized welfare state in the world, so that the high suicide rate can hardly be due to social insecurity. Moreover, as a report in the *American Sociological Review* points out, suicide rates tend to drop during wars. This is a further blow to the insecurity hypothesis. The conclusion would seem to be that too much security has the effect of slackening the vital tension and weakening the urge to live: a conclusion confirmed by Galbraith, who reports that after the RAF bombing raids on Hamburg in 1943 — raids in which between sixty thousand and a hundred thousand people were killed and half the city was burned to the ground — Hamburg's war production rose. The living standard of the workers had slumped, but

their efficiency was unimpaired. Insecurity made no difference.*

What attention should above all be focused on is the
state of mind that permeates an "affluent society." Men
clock in and clock out of work; they look at television
screens and go to see films based on best-selling novels.
The result is an increasing emphasis on man as a member
of society. John Donne's "No Man is an Island" becomes
a commonplace of the conventional wisdom, and the
Buddha's "Let each man be unto himself an island" is an
insight to be suspected and feared. There is a planing-
down process. Society comes first, the individual second.
This is not a consciously held notion in most people; it
is an attitude that comes naturally and infiltrates itself
into every aspect of the individual's work and recreation.

Inner-Direction and Other-Direction

In recent years, two American sociologists have published
important studies in this attitude, and I shall borrow from
their terminology. The first is David Riesman of Harvard,
whose essay *The Lonely Crowd* has the subtitle: "A Study
in the Changing American Character." The second is
William H. Whyte, whose book *The Organization Man* is
perhaps the most important study of the American character since De Tocqueville's *Democracy in America* was published over a century ago.

Riesman's book argues that there are three types of social

* Galbraith, of course, is not interested in this aspect of the matter. His
point is only that Hamburg's superfluous industries were destroyed, and
their man power freed for war production. "In reducing . . . the consumption of non-essentials . . . the attacks on Hamburg increased Germany's output of war material."

character, which he labels "tradition-directed," "inner-directed," and "other-directed." The society of the Middle Ages was mainly tradition-directed (that is, directed by ritual, social routine, religion). The inner-directed type of man is the man with pioneer qualities; in an expanding and changing society he can cope with the confusion because he possesses the self-discipline to drive towards a goal he has himself chosen. American literature in the nineteenth century is rich in this type: Thoreau, Emerson, Whitman, Dana, Poe.

BUT OUT OF SENSE THAT THE SOCIETY IS NOT GOING TOWARD BETTER

The other-directed man cares more for what the neighbors think than for what he wants in his own person; in fact, his wants eventually become synonymous with what the neighbors think. Riesman believes that American character is slowly changing from inner-directed to other-directed. The other-directed man demands security, and all his desires and ambitions are oriented towards society. Riesman writes of the other-directed man, *"other people are the problem"* (my italics).

Whyte's book, *The Organization Man,* is also a study in the increasing tendency to other-direction, but is particularly concerned with the man who works for a big-business organization. It demonstrates how the organization imposes an ethic of conformity on its employees. But this is not all. The terrifying part of this study is not merely the observation that men are willing to swallow the organization ethic; it is the fact that they swallow it *and like it.* Although the subject may sound narrower than that of *The Lonely Crowd,* Whyte's analysis actually ranges over every aspect of modern American life and culture.

These two books, like Vance Packard's *The Hidden Persuaders,* are arguing that the great danger is to over-

emphasize the social virtues until most men think of
nothing but "what the neighbors think." Whyte says, "I
am going to argue that he [the organization man] should
fight the organization. But not self-destructively. He may
tell the boss to go to hell, but he is going to have another
boss." In the same way, De Tocqueville had concluded
his study of democracy by acknowledging that democracy
has immense virtues and that these virtues will persist so
long as the balance is maintained between the spirit of
equality and the spirit of individualism. Riesman, Whyte,
Packard, Galbraith feel that the balance is now being lost
very quickly indeed. The necessity is to re-emphasize the
importance of inner-direction. Whyte suggests, with a
lightness of touch that should not be mistaken for flip-
pancy, that university research teams might take a rest
from studying how to fit the individual to the group and
try studying such topics as the tyranny of the happy-work
team, the adverse effects of high morale.

Whyte claims to show, among other things, that this
ethic of conformity is, in many ways, self-destructive.
For example: after devoting a great many pages to the
"testing of the organization man" (tests of intelligence
and conformity that have to be taken by candidates for
jobs), he goes on to reveal that when some of the bosses
took these tests they failed. The conclusion is not that the
bosses lacked the efficiency they demand from their employees, but that the qualities demanded of a boss have
very little to do with conformity, and a great deal to do
with individual drive and enterprise.

Meanwhile, the ethic of conformity steadily gains a
deeper hold. David Riesman has published an article
called "The Found Generation," an analysis of the aims

and ambitions of American college students. It reveals
that most American students possess the "organization mentality" to a degree that ought to gratify their future bosses.
Their ideas of the future have a monotonously similar
pattern: a home, a wife, a good job in some big organization (big organizations are "safer"), a car in two years, a
house in five, a large family, a wife who is a home-girl . . .
No interest whatever, he found, was shown in politics or
religion. Riesman comments that a world run by these
young people will be an eminently safe world; no one
will drop atom bombs or start world wars. But although
his comments have a professional detachment, he finds it
difficult to conceal his astonishment at the complete lack of
desire for adventure and of the feeling that the future is
full of vast yet undefined possibilities. He even intimates
that a similar cross section of his own generation (in the
early 1930's) would have yielded a very different result.

Neither Whyte nor Riesman, nor Packard, has any definite solution to offer. I have already quoted Whyte's suggestions. Packard concludes that "we can choose not to
be persuaded," and hopes that "this book may contribute
to the general awareness." Riesman put it like this:

. If the other-directed people should discover how much
needless work they do, discover that their own thoughts and
their own lives are quite as interesting as other people's, that,
indeed, they no more assuage their loneliness in a crowd of
peers than one can assuage one's thirst by drinking sea-water,
then we might expect them to become more attentive to
their own thoughts and aspirations.

But he has no suggestions as to how this might be brought
about. He writes oddly like Emerson, in the essay "Self-

Reliance"; but what can a self-reliant man do but urge others to become self-reliant?

Galbraith, as has already been noted, reaches conclusions that are purely economic, tending towards socialism. Socialism, however, though it might put an end to the consumer fallacy, can hardly be expected to go deeper. A novel like Dudintsev's *Not by Bread Alone* shows that Russia has the same kind of problems as America; in this case, the organization is the Soviet government and the bureaucracy it supports.

In fact, it is clear that, if one accepts the sociological method of Riesman and Whyte, it will be difficult to go beyond their conclusions. They end with a demand for more individualism; this could hardly be promoted by "social remedies," although social remedies might clear the way for a reassertion of it. If the question is one of remedies, it is back to the individual that the emphasis must be directed.

The real problem is the attitude of the individual towards himself. Riesman's conclusions about the Found Generation might indicate that the modern American college graduate is shrewd, sane, and well-adjusted, an altogether wiser man than those young people of thirty years ago, the Lost Generation, of whom Malcolm Cowley wrote in *Exile's Return*. But the case might also be that they are more afraid of insecurity than of boredom; that they are a browbeaten generation, lacking enterprise and a spirit of adventure. The point is a delicate one, and deserves closer scrutiny. It arises, for example, in *The Dialogues of Alfred North Whitehead* by Lucien Price. Whitehead had commented that English students seem better informed, more self-confident, than American students.

Price answered that this was because the cultural soil of
Europe is deeper. Whitehead disagreed. "You place too
much stress on soil. It isn't soil. You are the same people
as the Europeans. You have access to the whole of European history. *Americans are too diffident"* (my italics).
Whitehead offered no suggestion to account for this; he
simply observed it as a fact.

Kingsley Amis has recently commented that if the American male is "basically insecure," he makes a very good
job of concealing it. But perhaps insecurity is the wrong
word. What is in question is not so much insecurity as
a deeply ingrained habit of other-direction. The "insignificance" that De Tocqueville spoke of is not, however, a conscious inferiority complex: this species of self-mistrust is
taken too much for granted to qualify as a complex. It is
at once a man's attitude towards himself and his belief
about the world; it conceals, that is, a generalization about
mankind, a judgment about the stature of man. The other-
directed tend to divide the world into ordinary men and
extraordinary men. (Many European celebrities have
noticed the respect with which the American treats anyone who is regarded as extraordinary — the case of Dylan
Thomas offers a recent example.) The extraordinary man
seems to belong almost to a different species.

It is no accident that the Americans prefer to use the
word "genius" as an exclusive description rather than
adjectively. (Edison and Shakespeare were "geniuses," not
"men of genius.") When used adjectively, genius is a
quality that anyone might possess or attempt to develop;
on the other hand, one is born a genius as one might be
born with two heads. So the gulf between the ordinary and
the extraordinary is emphasized. This amounts to a funda-

mental self-depreciation: an other-direction that takes itself so much for granted that it has become a sort of self-
confidence. De Tocqueville had pointed this out in a
section in which he speaks of the high-flown language of
American politicians:

> I have frequently remarked that the Americans, who gen-
> erally treat of business in plain, clear language . . . are apt
> to become inflated as soon as they attempt a more poetical
> diction. They then vent their pomposity from one end of a
> harangue to the other. . . . The cause of this may be
> pointed out without much difficulty. In democratic com-
> munities, *each citizen is habitually engaged in contemplation
> of a very puny object, namely himself* [my italics]. If he ever
> raised his looks higher, he then perceives nothing but the im-
> mense form of society at large, or the still more imposing
> aspect of mankind. His ideas are all either extremely minute
> and clear, or extremely general and vague; what lies between
> is an open void.

The "realism" that, as De Tocqueville observed, makes
Americans "treat of business in plain, clear language" is
also the realism that makes the individual face his own
unimportance, a realism that prevents him from even
attempting anything extraordinary, since he acts upon
the premise that he is not extraordinary and never can be.
The result of this dubious realism (dubious because it
does not really face facts, but only a self-chosen set of
facts that lead to self-depreciation) is a loss of the drive
that comes from self-belief. There will be more to be
said of this attitude, as exemplified by American writers,
in a later section; for the moment, it is worth remarking
that one could hardly imagine a James Joyce or a Robert

Musil springing from an American background. In the case of both Joyce and Musil, there was an immense act of self-belief that had to sustain years of neglect. Both were born in small countries — Joyce in Ireland, Musil in Austria — where there was still a strong tradition of inner-direction. The disadvantages under which Joyce produced *Ulysses* and Musil *Der Mann ohne Eugenschaften* (*The Man without Qualities*) were great enough; imagine their case if an American upbringing had added to these all the weight of American diffidence and other-direction.

I have said that the unconscious assumptions that underlie other-direction conceal a generalization about mankind. An example may help to clarify my meaning. In his *Conversations with Goethe,* Eckermann tells how Goethe was asked what he would have done if he had been born in less fortunate circumstances, and, instead of "drawing the big prize" in the lottery, had "drawn a blank." Goethe replied: "Not everybody *is made for the big prize.* Do you think I should have done such a stupid thing as to draw a blank?"

Goethe's comment reveals more than a certainty of his own powers; it reveals a confidence about his luck, his destiny; the ancients would have put it that he was certain of the favor of the gods. Implied in his reply is an assumption about the relation between a man and his "destiny" (to use the term for want of a better). Such an assertion, indeed, has many implications. To begin with, it could never be based on the premise that man is a worm who longs for meaning and purpose in a universe that has neither; there is no sense of tragic irony here, no feeling of man's insignificance in a hostile or indifferent universe (as with Thomas Hardy). Nor does the remark "Not every-

body is made for the big prize" indicate that Goethe considered himself a different species from the rest of mankind; he was not a man to feel that he had achieved his
eminence by pure luck, by the accident of being born a
genius. On the contrary, it implies a denial of luck, a belief that, for the man who understands the workings of
destiny and trusts himself, eminence is only a matter of
hard work and determination.

What it comes to is this: in the simplest statement about
one's own nature there is an assumption about the whole
of humanity. A man need hold no conscious philosophy;
his attitude emerges from the whole texture of his everyday life. For this reason, a playwright like Arthur Miller
can say as much about American society in *Death of a
Salesman* as Riesman or Whyte can say in carefully docu-
mented social studies. Underlying the "success philosophy" that Miller puts into the mouth of Willy Loman,
there is a pessimistic assumption about Willy's own
stature and his relation to society. (Perhaps the success of
Death of a Salesman in the United States is a symptom of
an unconscious revolt against other-direction, just as the
slump in the sale of big cars in 1957 may indicate a revolt
against the "hidden persuaders.") And mention of Willy's
success philosophy suggests another interesting point: the
gradual change in the American conception of success.
Whyte uses the expression "Protestant ethic" for the
typical nineteenth-century success philosophy; "plenty of
room at the top," "don't be afraid to start on the bottom
rung," and so forth. But success in the twentieth century
involves being a good organization man, socially well-adjusted, and all the rest of it. The organization man is ex-

pected to be ambitious — but in a balanced, well-adjusted
way. Here is another aspect of the insignificance premise.
It is all very well for a James Joyce to possess the ambition
that eventually produces a *Ulysses,* because Joyce was born
a "genius"; but it would be improper, or just "cracked,"
for an "ordinary man" to set his ambitions on anything so
unusual.

Inner-Direction and Insanity

All this emerges very clearly in a case cited by the psychiatrist, Frederick Wertham, in his book *The Show of
Violence.* Robert Irwin had tried to amputate his penis.
He gave as his reason that he was attempting to kill his
sexual appetite, which, he believed, was stealing energy
from a far more important project. This project was
a rigorous dicipline of his own mind, with a view to
intensifying the power of his memory; for Irwin had
noted that the memory retains everything a man has ever
done or ever thought, and yet that only a minute part of
this store can be tapped and put to use. Irwin called his
discipline "visualizing." * But he had no particular skills,
and so was forced to take on the most frustrating and boring
of jobs; and after years of defeat he finally committed a
triple murder. This was not a case of sexual assault or
"irresistible impulse"; a suicidal impulse turned into a
gesture of disgust with society, the disgust of a man who
had been suffering from years of strain. The court rejected
Dr. Wertham's plea of insanity (rightly, perhaps), but

* His aim obviously has much in common with Proust's in *À la
Recherche du Temps Perdu.*

agreed so far as to impose a sentence of life imprisonment rather than of death.

Although Wertham tells the story with sympathy, he clearly considers Irwin insane in the fullest sense of the word, and his obsession with "visualizing" as sufficient evidence of this insanity. And yet it seems possible that if Irwin had been born, like Marcel Proust, of rich parents, his project might have led him to major creative achievement; at least, it would almost certainly not have led him to triple murder. But at no point in his narrative does Wertham appear to indicate that Irwin's visualizing might have been an obsession of the same type as that which led Joyce to write *Ulysses* or Columbus to discover America; and it is apparent that this was the general attitude of society towards Irwin's curiously touching concentration on his project.

I am not, of course, suggesting that if Irwin had been born in Ireland or Austria, instead of in Los Angeles, his obsession would have met with greater sympathy than in America or would have come to some kind of positive fruition. But there seems no reason to doubt that his American background was an additional handicap and contributed to his final defeat. Fanatical inner-direction is always regarded as a little "queer" by any society (until it has made itself respectable by visible success), but in America it would appear to be a sign of nothing less than insanity.

The same point is made by Whyte in a chapter called "The Fight Against Genius" (Chapter 16 of *The Organization Man*). After observing that recent years have witnessed an increasing emphasis on scientific teamwork and a suspicion of the "lone wolf" scientist, Whyte goes on to analyze the question of scientists in industry.* The only industrial laboratories that can boast "top scientists," he points out, are those that allow their researchers the maximum freedom; most big organizations distrust undirected research, and "to some management people, the desire to do free work is a downright defect, a symptom of maladjustment that demands cure. The failure to recognize the virtue of purposelessness," he continues, "is the starting point of industry's problem. . . . By its very nature, discovery has an accidental quality." He might have added that a certain element, not merely of independence but of downright anarchy, is necessary to the life of the creative worker. The kind of conformity now being demanded by the organization sounds, indeed, increasingly like some of the propaganda in *Brave New World*, with its motto, "Community, Identity, Stability"; and Whyte, when examining what happens when the organization tries to dominate not merely the employee but his family, too, actually evokes Orwell's *1984*, with its vision of totalitarian uniformity, and compares the tactics of the organization to those of Big Brother. The fact is that although Huxley's *Brave New World*, Orwell's *1984*, and Zamyatin's *We* are all satires on communism, their line of attack has a great deal of relevance to the organization. Nor have we in England any reason to congratulate ourselves on the idea that our insularity and tradition of personal independence make the warnings of *The Organization Man* and *The Hidden Persuaders* irrelevant. The trends may be less advanced over here, but they are here all the same. In

* Negley Farson has pointed out to me that Sinclair Lewis' *Arrowsmith* (1926) contains a remarkable anticipation of *The Organization Man* in its chapters describing the conflict between the idealistic scientist, Arrowsmith, and the publicity-loving head of the corporation.

"A Note on Billy Graham" in his collection of essays, *Thoughts in the Wilderness,* J. B. Priestley finishes by observing: "The truth is that now the British crowd is more easily enticed and dominated by mass-communication, showmanship and ballyhoo than the American crowd is. The Americans have had a great deal more of it, and for years were far more responsive to it, but while there is in them still a strain of the gullible and hysterical, there is also the work of a powerful antibody, the strain of the sceptical. . . . The satirical journalist and the jeering comic are figures of power in America. . . . But the newly arrived British . . . are bowled over by the new nonsense as easily as the Martian invaders, in Wells's story, fell victim to the strange bacteria of the world. Their minds are wide open as well as being empty." And Mr. Priestley's talk of empty minds is surely only another way of observing that the English, like the Americans, are changing their character and being other-directed instead of inner-directed. His essay, on the other hand, suggests a ray of hope: namely, that some process of resistance may be unconsciously going forward, and may blaze up as revolt before the 1984 stage is reached. But perhaps, at this stage, it is more politic to ignore the hope and concentrate on the danger.

Other-Directed Religion

Apropos of Billy Graham, it might be of interest to glance at the religious revivals of our age. Graham himself is a depressing symptom of other-direction, and his immense success in England is one more sign that we are not far behind the Americans in a character change that will make Riesman's *The Lonely Crowd* as applicable here as there. His evangelistic methods consist of straightforward Bible-bashing; when Whitehead said, "Religion is what a man does with his own solitariness," he was not thinking of the Billy Graham variety. I have attended only one of Graham's meetings at Harringay. The show had the quality of a high-standard American musical. The music was syncopated, jazzy; the hymns sounded no more like the hymns we sang at school than Bing Crosby's "I'm Dreaming of a White Christmas" sounds like a Christmas carol. Graham's preaching had a colloquial freshness, an easy man-to-man appeal, that fitted in with the high quality of the rest of the show, and imposed no strain on the listener. He retold some parable from the New Testament (I cannot now remember which, though I do remember his explanation that a "publican" was the equivalent of a modern gangster), emphasized that heaven and salvation were round the corner for every single one of his audience, and glossed lightly over the "burning pit" that would be the lot of those others who failed to take advantage of his offer. By this time the singing was like something out of *Showboat,* and Graham invited converts to come forward and be accepted into the arms of Jesus.*

Graham's appeal, as far as I could judge, consisted in giving his audience (who had been steeling themselves for a chunk of old-fashioned Methodism) an unexpectedly

* I was so interested that I accepted his invitation, and was shown into a large tent in the rear of the building, where a Welsh clergyman with thick spectacles read the Bible to me, and then asked — with sudden penetration — if I was doing it "for a lark." I answered, with perfect truthfulness, that I was not, regarding my scientific curiosity as wholly serious.

pleasant evening and then utilizing the good will that
resulted for his man-to-man plea that they should come
forward and be saved. The effect of the show was that of
a large whiskey. The preaching aimed solely at suggesting
that Christianity was a simple, obvious way of "getting
right with God" and going to heaven, while Graham's
boyish charm and colloquial language combined with the
soothing music to make the listener feel that religion was
no more remote and otherworldly than his favorite television program. Here was the technique of mass media —
films and TV — applied to conversion. It depended for
its success, as J. B. Priestley has observed, upon the re-
ceptivity of its film-and-television-trained audience and
upon the emptiness of their minds.

Of the other religious sects of our time, Jehovah's Witnesses, one of the most successful, rely in the same way on
the emptiness of their converts. Unlike the Quakerism
preached by George Fox, their creed knows nothing of an
"inner light." Again, my interest in this sect led me to
attend some of their meetings. I was chiefly struck by
their emphasis on the "Law." Whole meetings were devoted to discussing the Law as laid down in the Old Testament and to insisting on rigorous obedience to its letter.
Their appeal (if such a militant demand can be called an
appeal) depended on their assertion that the Day of Judgment would occur within the lifetime of people alive in
1914, (that is, before 1990) and that only Jehovah's Witnesses would be saved. I was reminded irresistibly of
Peter Verkovensky, in Dostoevsky's *The Devils*, who
gained converts for his revolution by assuring them that
it was already organized and would inevitably take place
within the next few months, and by implying that liquida-

tion awaited anyone who declined the invitation. The Witnesses made no call to inner-direction. Everything had been laid down in the Bible; salvation consisted in allowing oneself to be completely and unreservedly dominated by it — or rather by the extraordinary interpretations they put upon it.* As to the Day of Judgment, no one seemed to be aware that two earlier Judgment Days (as predicted by Judge Russell, the founder) had arrived and passed without incident.

There is, I think, no need to emphasize further that these "religious revivals" depend upon a complete lack of inner-direction on the part of their converts: upon an appeal, in fact, to authority. This explains the power of Frank Buchman's Moral Rearmament movement, with its emphasis on society (especially "high society"), and the esoteric appeal of the British Israelites, who apparently believe that the British race is a descendant of the ten lost tribes of Israel.

In all these cases, the organization that seeks to dominate is a religious organization; otherwise, the pattern is the same as in the secular organization, and the observations of Whyte and Riesman are confirmed. The inner light, like Riesman's inner direction, is out. Kierkegaard's "Truth is subjectivity" has no relevance here, for the people concerned possess no subjectivity, or none to speak of. It is merely a matter of plunging into the mystique of

---

* I discover a typical example in today's *Daily Express* (15-12-58). A baby was about to die of a rare blood disease, and only a blood transfusion could save its life. But the parents, who were Jehovah's Witnesses, refused to permit it, on the grounds that the Bible forbids it. The father quoted the Acts of the Apostles (XV, 28-29) : "That ye abstain from meat offered to idols and from blood." The fact that the text refers to *blood-drinking* was unable to shake the resolution of the parents. A Toronto judge ordered that the baby should be removed from the parents' custody.

the community (in this case, the "little flock of Jesus"). Religion as a highly organized and concentrated form of inner-direction is disappearing in the twentieth century. If religion is "what the individual does with his solitude," then the definition excludes these mass movements. There has been no religious revival in our time.

The American Child

In *The Hidden Persuaders* Packard has a chapter on "The Psycho-Seduction of Children" that sounds some of his most ominous notes. He tells how advertisers set out to make contact with American children, who can not only persuade their parents to buy the advertised products but also help to spread the names of products by getting advertising songs off by heart. Riesman has commented that the advertisers think of their juvenile audience as a potential army of highly trained consumers. Nor is their value limited to potential buying: Packard states that "the Davy Crockett craze of 1955, which gave birth to 300 Davy Crockett products, lured $3,000,000,000 from American pockets."

The implications are disturbing, and one in particular. So long as this deliberate cultural cheapening continues to pay, so long will the mass manipulators remain actively opposed to any rise in the cultural standard of television and films. A recent case in point was the affair of the horror comics. Their suppression, as Dr. Frederick Wertham's book on the subject, *Seduction of the Innocent*, suggests unmistakably, was no mere outbreak of unrealistic American puritanism, on a par with Prohibition and the activities of sundry anti-vice societies. The examples he cites are nauseating; their constant preoccupation with cruelty and brutality could produce nothing in a child but callous and anti-social emotions. It nevertheless took years to suppress these publications effectively. They were making too much money for too many people.

An audience of children can be manipulated far more easily by advertisers than an audience of adults, the reason being that *all* children are other-directed. All children base their lives and conduct on the insignificance hypothesis: the world belongs to adults. A world in which all adults had some of the characteristics of children would be an advertiser's dream. But in point of fact this is the world that is now coming into existence, the world of Riesman's and Whyte's observation. It is a world in which the organization and society at large play precisely the role in the life of the American adult that the adult plays in the life of the child.

There is an essential unreality in the relationship between a child and an adult. A sympathetic and imaginative adult might just possibly be able to see into the mind of a child, but the child can never have any true knowledge of the world of the grownup. And usually neither can fully comprehend the other. In a tradition-directed society, this void of unreality is taken for granted. The child has to struggle to enter the world of the adult and is usually "kept in his place," with the result, very frequently, that he retains his attitude of submission to authority well into adulthood. In a recent lecture tour of German universities, I noticed that German students tend to be less questioning, and far less obstreperous, than English students. The reason for this, I was told, lies in the strictness of the school training of the German child; the authority

of schoolmasters is absolute until the children are well
into their teens. Even with advanced students, freedom
is not encouraged as much as it is in England and America.

But however many disadvantages this system may have,
it also has advantages, as comparison with American conditions makes clear. From an early age the American child
tends to be given considerable freedom; so much so that
certain alarmed observers have spoken of America as a ^
child-dominated country. (This also explains why advertisers find the American child such excellent material.)
A journalist friend who recently returned from America
commented on the frequency of cases in which children
have murdered their parents — because they were for-
bidden to use the car, or to listen to a certain television
program, or for some equally trivial motive. These examples are not, of course, cited to argue for or against any
particular theory of education. They are offered only as
extreme indications of something that must have been
apparent to observers of the American scene for many
years: that the American child is treated far more like an ⌐
adult than the European child. Democracy is being ex-
tended to the world of the moppets. The void of unreality that must exist between the mind of the adult and
that of the child is *symbolized* by adult authority, in the ⌐
same way that in Christianity the relation between man
and God is symbolized by certain rituals. But the relationship is an imponderable; it cannot be seen and touched.
In America, it would seem that democratic thinking has
led to a feeling that adult authority has no more foundation in fact than church ritual, and there is thus a tendency
to behave as if the void did not exist. The child is assumed
to have a far greater capacity for freedom than it may, in

actuality, possess. The result is a blurring of the child-adult relationship. A child is granted the same right of self-expression as an adult; thus, the violence and irrationality of the child are carried into the world of action, instead of remaining in the world of fantasy, and lead, in extreme cases, even to murder.

The reason for this is not far to seek. There is more emphasis on child guidance and child psychology in America than in Europe. Most Americans have a considerable respect for the figure of the psychologist — in fact, for any kind of scientist. American magazines devote a great deal of space to articles on "How to Bring Up Your Child," usually by psychologists. Far more books are published yearly in America on this subject than in England. The American attitude to children is part of the general American attitude to scientific authority. The psychiatrist seems to play a far larger part in cases of juvenile delinquency, and criminal cases generally, in America than in Europe.*

I have tried to argue that this diffidence, which seems to lie at the root of the attitude of the American towards children, is based on a certain failure of *realism*. There is a void between the mind of the adult and that of the child. A realistic approach would recognize this and accept the responsibility that it implies, the need for au-

* At the time of writing, I am living in Cornwall, where the opposite attitude can be plainly seen. In a recent case in which a youth murdered both his parents, and threw their bodies over a cliff, the evidence of a psychiatrist testifying to his complete instability and mental confusion — a testimony that would almost certainly have secured his release in America — had the opposite effect on a Cornish jury, who showed their contempt for it by finding him guilty of first-degree murder. It seems probable that without the psychiatrist's testimony a verdict of "Insane" might have been returned.

thority. It is the same kind of failure of realism that Barrie
satirizes in *The Admirable Crichton,* where the socialist
Lord Loam has the servants in to tea.

The Pattern of Violence

In his study of American juvenile delinquency, *The
Shook-Up Generation,* Harrison Salisbury suggests that the
violence of the New York street gangs is perhaps only a
reflection of the violence of the modern world. The pattern of their lives is influenced not only by television plays
about gangsters and films like *Blackboard Jungle* and
Rebel Without a Cause, but also by international tensions,
the cold war, the threat of atomic warfare. The steep rise
in juvenile delinquency since the war is usually attributed
to the broken homes and the sense of instability caused
by that social upheaval. And yet it is difficult to believe
that this is the whole explanation. War or no war, modern
society was becoming increasingly mechanized. The organization mentality now makes itself felt long before most
teen-agers have left school. This in itself is not the direct
cause of teen-age revolt; German children were brought
up to be army-minded, and the army is another organization; nevertheless, juvenile delinquency in Germany before the war was a good deal lower than after it. But
military organization depends upon discipline; business
ethics is based upon anarchy, shrewdness, and enterprise,
the "grab what you can get" system. The American teen-
ager lives in a society that overawes him with its power and
wealth, and that tries to browbeat him with the "organization ethic." And the American educational system, as I
have already commented, attempts to teach its pupils to

be self-determined at an early age. As Harrison Salisbury points out, the youths who hang around in drugstores today and listen to jazz, or who steal a car to drive to a dance hall a hundred miles away, might have joined a sailing ship to make the run around the Horn a century ago. Adolescence is the time when a desire for inner-direction begins to stir and is not yet held in check by realism. All this contributes to a revolt that lacks direction. This revolt is the essential intermediate stage between the ambitious imaginings of childhood and the adult's "realistic" surrender to the organization. Salisbury has commented that most of the youths who belong to slum gangs would like to escape from the slums into more decent lives, but that most of them lack the will power needed for the hard struggle it would involve (as well as having no idea of how to go about it).

This problem is not, of course, confined to America. In England, statistics for juvenile delinquency in 1951 had doubled the figure for 1937; 1951 was a peak year, but the figures are still a great deal higher than before the war. Russia also has her "teddy boys," the *stilyagi,* although their activities are less violent than those of American delinquents; they confine themselves to wearing American-style clothes (especially colored ties) and listening to American jazz. The brief outbreaks of teen-age violence in Russia after the war were quickly suppressed by armed troops, who were given instructions to fire at any crowds of teen-agers on the streets. The Russian teddy boy, like his American counterpart, is sullen and rebellious about attempts to make him social-minded and professes bored indifference to communist ideology. His attitude shows the same callow and unrealistic attempt to be inner-directed.

He is still in the stage of feeling a certain instinctive rebellion against the insignificance that society is trying to
impose upon him. When he learns to accept it, he will
be a "good member of society."

The Psychology of Violence

The rise in juvenile delinquency has been accompanied
by a rise in the crime and suicide rates in many countries
since the war. In England, 1951 was a peak year for most
types of crime; the figures were between two and three
times those of the pre-war period. Since then, there has
been a slight decline in most types of crime. Crimes of
violence and sexual offenses have, however, continued to
rise steadily, and in 1955 the number of sexual offenses
committed in England and Wales was 17,000, as compared
to 5000 before the war. Plainly, the war cannot be entirely
to blame, for the tendency is becoming steadily more
marked.

The causes are probably too complex to submit to generalization. Nevertheless, it seems plausible that one of the
causes might be sought in the increasing trend of other-
direction. It is known, for example, that an enormous
number of violent psychopaths show the same character
pattern: their long periods of submission to a sense of inferiority (or "ordinariness") are broken by sudden violence. It would seem that there is something about a life
lived on a general level of insignificance that makes for
outbreaks of violence. This violence may be directed
against the self or against society; that is, may result in
suicide or in crime. Suicide would appear to be the ultimate expression of self-contempt, and the violence that

often accompanies it probably springs from the same cause. (The *American Sociological Review* survey, already quoted, reveals that one third of the suicides among un-skilled workers are accompanied by murder; this is six times the rate among the white-collar class of suicide.) All this points to the idea that the increased other-direction in modern society, and the sense of insignificance that goes with it, may be one of the causes behind the increased crime rate.

This would certainly account for the fact that sexual crimes have shown the steepest rate of increase over the past ten years. Sex and the idea of other-direction are bound closely together. Other-direction is a strong sense of society, of laws and taboos, a sense of constant responsibility to the other people. Inner-direction tends to channel the energies of the individual; other-direction relies on social outlets for them. For all men of strong sexual appetites, any woman is a potential partner. The inner-directed man tends to select his sexual partner (or partners), since selec-tion and purpose are implicit in his inner-direction; other-direction tends to destroy selectivity, to increase passivity. (This can be seen in the case of television addicts, who sit in front of their sets waiting to be entertained, indifferent to what they are watching as long as they are watching something.) Consequently, although all women are poten-tially sexual partners, the other-directed man is keenly aware of the social taboos that prevent his desires from find-ing satisfaction. If he revolts against his sense of insignifi-cance, his lack of inner-direction, the revolt will tend to express itself as a defiance of taboos, a deliberate contra-vention of laws, in a crime of violence or a sexual offense. (When the hero of Henri Barbusse's *L'Enfer* says, "It is not a woman I want: it is all women," he is expressing the typical attitude of the bewildered other-directed man.)

The case histories of many psychopaths suggest that the other-directed man may release his frustrated desire for inner-direction in a sudden act of violence. A clear example is the case of Peter Kurten, the Düsseldorf sadist, who confessed after his arrest that he had often walked through the streets of Düsseldorf entertaining daydreams of blowing up the whole city with dynamite. Professor Berg, the psychologist who examined Kurten in prison and wrote the classic study of his case, dismissed the hypothesis that Kurten's crimes sprang from a revenge-mania against society, on the grounds that Kurten later revealed their sexual origin. But if the theory that other-direction makes for sudden violence has any validity, there is nothing incompatible between the two motives.

In other ways, Kurten provides verification of the theory. He was known to his neighbors and workmates as a "quiet, insignificant little man," and for long after his arrest they continued to believe that the police had made a mistake. They found it impossible to associate him with the series of murders and violent attacks of which he was accused. What none of them knew was that he had spent nearly the whole of his adult life in prison, much of it in solitary confinement. (He was forty-eight when he was executed.)

What emerges clearly from Professor Berg's study is that Kurten was a man of rare intelligence and honesty, who was deeply interested in his own case and in the urges that led him to kill. He had been brought up against the worst kind of slum background, in a setting of sexual depravity (his father was given a prison sentence for raping Kurten's sister), and had early been taught the pleasures of inflicting pain by a sadistic dogcatcher. In his long periods of solitary confinement, Kurten, with little else to do, would amuse himself with sexual fantasies that, stimulated by an increasing grudge against society, became steadily more violent.

Under better social conditions, Kurten might have emerged as an intelligent inner-directed person. But, as with Robert Irwin, his inner-direction was constantly frustrated, in his case by a society that exacted long periods of imprisonment as a penalty for his petty crimes. The effect of these periods of frustration and boredom was to destroy his sense of inner-direction.

The circumstances of Kurten's arrest also tend to verify this interpretation. When he suspected that the police net was closing in on him, he confessed to his wife. She also had had no suspicion of his double life. When he had convinced her, he urged her to give him up and claim the reward money. While he was still engaged in persuading her, he took her out to supper. She could not eat. He finished his share, then ate hers, too. The prospect of arrest stimulated his appetite. The same thing happened on the night before his execution; then he ate an enormous condemned-cell supper and asked for a second helping. Excitement — even the excitement of his own arrest or execution — stimulated his vital functions, including his appetite.

The craving for excitement *at any cost* (even of misfortune to oneself) is a sign of undeveloped emotions. *And an undeveloped inner life is equivalent to other-direction.* Kurten's life of crime was, I would suggest, a result of this urge for stimulation, for escape from other-direction to the temporary heightened intensity of inner-direction. He was a man whose basic need was for inner-direction, who lacked the strength to gain it by intellectual or emotional discipline, and who threw the whole weight of his need for intensity upon his body. But this burden of longing for intensity cannot be borne by the body, which is easily exhausted and demands stronger and stronger stimuli.* Under different circumstances, Kurten might equally well have become an alcoholic or a drug addict.

It seems likely that the reason why "insignificant" men become capable of violent crimes is that the need for inner-direction becomes suddenly overpowering. The psychopath, lacking intellectual or emotional means of achieving it, throws the burden on his physical appetites. As a person who spends most of his life in an other-directed state, he has no other resources.

I have so far spoken of inner-directed and other-directed types as though some people could be clearly labeled inner-directed and others other-directed. But obviously this is not so. Everyone is a combination of the two types. Riesman admits this in *The Lonely Crowd,* when he says: "the types of character and society dealt with in this book are *types;* they do not exist in reality, but are a construction, based on a selection of certain historical problems." It may be true that many people spend their lives in a state of more or less contented other-direction; that others (rarer) have achieved a certain stability of inner-direction; while a third group, basically inner-directed, spend their lives in a state of other-direction with sudden violent out-

---

* De Sade himself recognized this as the root cause of sadism. In *Les 120 Journées de Sodome,* the libertine Durcet says: "One need only be mildly jaded, and all these infamies assume a richer meaning: satiety inspires them. . . . One grows tired of the commonplace, the imagination becomes vexed, and the slenderness of our means, the weakness of our faculties, the corruption of our souls lead us to these abominations." Vol. II, p. 16, Olympia Press edition.

breaks of rebellion to achieve flashes of inner-direction, after which they may relapse contentedly back to other-direction for a long spell.

Huxley, Orwell, and Zamyatin have all portrayed a society of contented other-directed types; but it is doubtful whether many such people exist outside fiction. The real difference between people is the degree to which they are other-directed or inner-directed. And these terms may cover a host of finer shades that, for the moment, defy definition.

Yet the facts are there to be explained, and until a more subtle hypothesis proves its value, these approximations with all their clumsiness are indispensable. And there would seem to be some connection between other-direction, an assumption of diffidence (or insignificance), and a periodic revolt against it that often expresses itself in violence. If this connection exists, then it may also explain why a society whose character is changing from inner-direction to other-direction builds up a need for violent self-expression which may, under certain circumstances, express itself in wars. I submit this hypothesis as a stopgap until a better one replaces it, which is the role of all hypotheses.

Conclusion

The total result of a study of Galbraith, Riesman, Whyte and Packard is deeply disturbing. Moreover, their observations are relevant not for America alone; America is merely ahead of Europe in the deindividualizing process. Riesman states that the increase of other-direction is associated with "a shift from an age of production to an age of consumption," and Galbraith and Packard show the same concern with the dangers of the "consumer fallacy." But although some of Galbraith's remedies point towards socialism (being an American, he takes care not to go that far), there is no reason to suppose that socialism is a panacea, as the evidence of Soviet Russia will show. The problem centers upon the deleterious effects of *any* organization ethic. The harsh truth would appear to be that as far as other-direction goes, there is not much to choose between Russia and the United States except that American sociologists are allowed to point out the dangers, while it is doubtful whether a Russian would have the same freedom. The fact that Whyte can evoke Orwell's *1984* in writing of American business organizations speaks for itself. "De Tocqueville made a prophecy. If America ever destroyed its genius, it would be by intensifying the social virtues at the expense of the others, by making the individual come to regard himself as a hostage to prevailing opinion, by creating, in sum, a tyranny of the majority." It makes no difference whether this tyranny calls itself totalitarianism or democracy.

This is not, of course, to attack the system of representative government. On the contrary, the analyses of Riesman, Whyte, and others make it plain that this is the only final defense against the development of the inner totalitarianism of big business. The need is to check the process of deindividualization, and this requires a balance of forces. There must always be an opposition. Without it, the force that predominates becomes a form of totalitarianism in the limits within which it operates. If the big-business organizations of America are preferable to the communist governments, this is only because they are not yet in a position to dominate the whole community. But the tendency increases. A recent publication, *The Exploding Metropolis*, by the editors of *Fortune* (of whom Whyte is one), considers the problem of the spreading American city almost as if the words "city" and "organization" were synonymous. Whyte complains of the process of deindividualization that is now altering the face of New York: the uniform skyscrapers and apartment buildings which are replacing the back streets, the Italian restaurants and small movie theaters, the grimy tenements and Victorian houses, and all the different atmospheres and appearances that make up a city's individuality. Whyte is not arguing against slum clearance. He is arguing that social progress does not *have* to mean crushing uniformity. It is still a problem of balance.

In England we have some reason for congratulating ourselves on the amount of inner-direction that still exists. We are more socialistic than America and less than Russia; there is always an Opposition in the House of Commons. But this may only be because of the fact that Britain's resources are smaller than those of the United States, that the drift towards the organization ethic is therefore slower, and that the drift is also opposed by a stronger tendency to tradition-direction in England. But no one can seriously deny that the tendency is there, and that it is increasing. And no one can read Riesman and Whyte — or even De Tocqueville — without feeling that what is being said has a very considerable relevance for England as well as for the United States. The danger may be ten years more advanced in America, but that hardly gives us reason for complacency.

How far, in fact, does England — or Europe, for that

matter — show the same tendencies to other-direction as America? No English sociologists have published studies that compare with *The Lonely Crowd* or *The Organization Man*. But both Riesman and Whyte have shown how American culture has come to reflect the organization mentality. A comparison of the recent literature of America with that of Europe leads to some interesting observations.

Part Two

The Evidence
of Literature

No poetry can bloom in the arid modern soil, the drama has died, and the patrons of art are no longer even conscious of shame at profaning the most sacred of ideals. The ecstatic dream, which some 12th century monk cut into the stones of the sanctuary hallowed by the presence of his God, is reproduced to bedizen a warehouse.

BROOKS ADAMS: *The Law of Civilization and Decay,* 1896

تعاونوا على البرّ والتقوى ولا تعاونوا على الاثم والعدوان

دوّهٔ‎

HOW FAR does the study of literature — particularly of plays and novels — bear out the analyses of Riesman and Whyte? Whyte himself has glanced at this aspect of the matter in *The Organization Man*. The section on "The Organization Man in Fiction" is one of the shortest in the book and deals chiefly with cheap magazine fiction, but there is an interesting study of Herman Wouk's best seller, *The Caine Mutiny*.

The central incident of *The Caine Mutiny* is the one-man mutiny of the first officer, Maryk, against the neurotic Captain Queeg. Over a period of months it has become increasingly obvious to the crew that Queeg is slightly in- *محبوب‎* sane, or at least unbalanced. But his neuroses, although they impose humiliation and nervous strain on the crew, do not become dangerous until the *Caine* runs into a storm when in convoy. Queeg loses his nerve and tries to run the ship away from the storm. Maryk knows that their only chance of not being swamped is to turn the ship and run her head on into the wind. With immense reluctance he tells Queeg that he is relieving him of his command under Article 184, "for medical reasons," and orders the ship to be turned into the wind. Later, they pass the upturned hull of a destroyer that had apparently tried Queeg's running-away tactics.

Maryk is court-martialed. The defense lawyer, Greenwald, succeeds in making it obvious that Queeg is unbalanced. Maryk is acquitted, and Queeg's career is ruined. But at this point, Wouk turns the tables. At a dinner in which the *Caine* officers celebrate Maryk's acquittal, Greenwald makes a speech in which he tells Maryk that he would have preferred to defend Queeg, that Maryk was in the wrong for opposing his officer, and that the real villain of the piece was Keefer, a malcontent intellectual who had incited Maryk to rebel. I quote Whyte's analysis: "In what must be the most irrelevant climax in contemporary fiction, Greenwald says that he is a Jew, and that his grandmother was boiled down for soap in Germany, and that thanks be to the Queegs who kept the ships going. He throws a glass of champagne at Keefer."

Queeg represents the navy; in time of war it is the business of all officers to make the best of their commanders and keep the ships sailing. This, apparently, is the author's view. But, as Whyte points out, the author does not go into what would have happened if Maryk had not turned the ship into the wind, and it had met the same fate as the destroyer.

Whyte wondered whether the public who made *The Caine Mutiny* a best seller, or who saw the film or the play based upon it, understood its fundamental argument. He set the book as the subject of a school essay. The analyses left no doubt that the main theme had been grasped. But what was astounding was the fact that fifteen out of sixteen students sided with Herman Wouk — against Maryk, for Queeg. A typical sentence from one of the essays was: "I believe that one should obey orders, no matter what the circumstances." Whyte is obviously astonished, and speculates that twenty years ago more students would have voted for Maryk.

The same tendency can be seen in another recent best-selling novel, *From Here to Eternity,* by James Jones. Although the plot of the novel centers upon Prewett, an ex-boxer who refuses to enter the company boxing team and in consequence is subjected to a long course of petty indignities, there is no suggestion that Prewett is the rugged individualist who stands out against the organization — in this case, the American army. On the contrary, he loves the army. When his girl asks him why he intends to go back after a period of AWOL, he finds her anger incomprehensible:

> "What did the army ever do for you besides beat you up and treat you like scum and throw you in jail like a criminal? What do you want to go back for?"
>
> "What do I want to go back for?" Prewett said, wonderingly, "I'm a soldier."

It is not the army that he opposes, but only the attempt to force him to box. He knows that there is nothing in army regulations that forces him to box. But he also knows that there is nothing in army regulations to stop Captain Holmes from giving him hell, and he accepts this without protest.

This is the more astonishing because a casual reader might suppose that the book was intended to be a denunciation of the army. The author makes it plain that he is aware that the army robs men of individuality. When

Sergeant Warden decides to seduce Captain Holmes's wife, Mr. Jones writes:

> He still knew that he would do it, not as vengeance, or even retribution, but as an expression of himself, *to regain the individuality* that Holmes and the rest of them, unknowingly, had taken from him. And he understood suddenly why a man who has lived his whole life working for a corporation might commit suicide simply to express himself, would foolishly destroy himself because it was the only way to prove his own existence [my italics].

But it soon becomes apparent that the author's attitude towards the army is as favorable as Wouk's towards the navy (a fact that the reader might be led to suspect from the dedication of the book to the United States Army). He even seems to accept the brutality without condemnation:

> There was a satisfaction that came from having borne pain that nothing else could ever quite equal, even though the pain was philosophically pointless and never affected anything but the nervous system. Physical pain made its own justification.

It is the same with the other characters. In the film of the book, Captain Holmes is cashiered for his villainies, but this would appear to be foreign to the author's intention. In the novel, Holmes simply moves to another company in the course of promotion, and is not heard of again. Even Staff Sergeant Judson, one of the novel's most unpleasant characters, is depicted with a detached insight that comes closely to sympathy. He had beaten a man to death in the stockade, and Prewett had vowed to kill him. As he dies, Judson expresses a kind of innocence:

"You've killed me. Why'd you want to kill me?" he said, and died. The expression of hurt surprise and wounded reproach and sheer inability to understand stayed on his face.

It says a great deal for Jones's power as a writer that the reader accepts his attitude towards the army for as long as he is reading the book. Good writing can induce a suspension of the reader's normal beliefs and sympathies. But there is a difference between accepting Jones's views while one reads his novel and accepting them as a system of practical belief.

The Caine Mutiny and *From Here to Eternity* are examples in which a particular organization is the real hero. But frequently in recent American fiction, society itself, or the socially well-adjusted man, is the hero. An interesting example in this genre is *By Love Possessed,* by James Gould Cozzens, and its interest is heightened by the fact that its author is a New England traditionalist, who has much in common with T. S. Eliot. Its hero, Arthur Winner, is a middle-aged lawyer whose chief virtues are tolerance, kindness, shrewdness, an ability to handle people and make them trust him. The book has its positive and negative aspects. Positively, it is a careful picture of a man whom Mr. Cozzens obviously admires for possessing all the social virtues; Winner is the perfectly adjusted member of society. Negatively, it is an attack on many things that Mr. Cozzens seems to dislike: industrialism, Catholicism, foreign immigrants, jiving teen-agers and their taste in music and literature and popular entertainers. Cozzens's Brocton seems as idyllic and "olde worlde" as Hawthorne's Boston, and about as out of date. But what mainly emerges from the novel is Mr. Cozzens's portrait of the well-adjusted Social

Man, the man with a genius for human relationships, a sort of blueprint of what the students of Riesman's Found Generation would all like to be at fifty-five. The only thing Winner lacks, Cozzens implies, is a little humility about his goodness, and this is supplied at the end of the novel, when he decides to condone a fraud (a situation Granville-Barker had already exploited in *The Voysey Inheritance*). But even this is not really an act of defying society; it is only a deepened realization that men must be tolerant of one another's faults, and that the best way to serve society may be to conspire to deceive it. Society, in Cozzens's view, comes first and last; *By Love Possessed* is an epic of humanistic thought.

This tendency to make a town or a city, rather than any particular individual, the hero of a book has become an accepted tradition in American literature since Sinclair Lewis' *Main Street* and Sherwood Anderson's *Winesburg, Ohio*. In books of this kind there is usually a central character to hold the book together, but the emphasis, as their titles often imply, is upon the town. In William Faulkner, a whole county is constructed as the "hero" of a series of novels. (The title of Faulkner's latest book is, significantly, *The Town*.) Although many of the novels have some sort of hero, it is obvious that Faulkner thinks of himself as a historian of an imaginary county rather than as a writer about certain trends in individual characters that interest him.

The Defeated Hero

Faulkner's work also runs into another important area of American writing: the study of the defeated man. Faulkner implies that a heroic age has gone — the age of the Civil War, of his Colonel Sartoris and General Compson — and that a new age of petty, calculating little men (the Snopeses) is coming in. His early work is largely concerned with the defeat and disappearance of the remnants of the heroic tradition. He admires, in the modern world, minor, unheroic figures who "endure" — like Lena Grove in *Light in August* and Dilsey in *The Sound and the Fury*. There is no heroism left.

Another writer whose work overlaps many boundaries is John Dos Passos. *Manhattan Transfer* is an early experiment in the Beat Generation tradition. Its hero is mainly the city of New York, but at the end of the book one of its focal characters thumbs a lift and moves on, not caring where the truck takes him. But in his immense trilogy, *U.S.A.* (of which, as one might suppose, America is the hero), one of the few sympathetic and idealistic characters, Charley Anderson, has a slow moral disintegration and meets a violent death. In *Three Soldiers,* similarly, the sensitive musician, John Andrews, is finally shot for desertion. In Dos Passos, when society is not the hero (or the villain), the hero is defeated.

Modern American drama provides complete corroboration of Riesman's theories. Its major figure, Eugene O'Neill, has written constantly of defeat. In *The Hairy Ape,* the central character, a powerfully built stoker who represents primeval human energy and values, finds that he is helpless when he clashes with society. As he shouts his disgust, the people walking past ignore him; when he attacks them, they walk on untouched. In the contest of individual versus society, the individual has to learn that "you can't win." O'Neill's plays are full of bewildered

WHAT YOUR PLACE IN SOCIETY! p. 46

characters driven by their passions, and the ending is
nearly always despair and defeat. It is difficult to imagine
anyone going further in pessimism than O'Neill does in
The Iceman Cometh, which portrays a group of down-
and-outs in a waterfront dive, living off illusions. The
source of all this gloom seems to be the feeling, so clearly
expressed in *The Hairy Ape,* that the individual will
always be crushed and defeated by society.

The same is true of the plays of Tennessee Williams,
which have been described by Professor Allan G. Halline as
"true to the modern spirit of unrelieved failure or disaster."
Williams's drama is built on two character types: shrink-
ing, dreamy introverts and powerful force-of-nature creatures. The introverts can never come to terms with the
world: this is so in all his work, from *The Glass Menagerie*
to *Cat on a Hot Tin Roof.* But if the introverts are defeated by modern life, the force-of-nature characters do not
seem to be much better off. Big Daddy, in *Cat on a Hot
Tin Roof,* is dying of cancer. The dynamic Pole, Kowalsky,
in *A Streetcar Named Desire,* is tied to the life of a slum
tenement and an atmosphere of futility. A bare plot analysis of the plays of Williams would give a casual reader the
impression that "Williams" is one of O'Neill's pseudonyms
(except, perhaps, for Williams's interest in homosexuality).
Both playwrights deal mainly with ordinary people, violent
passions, and defeat. Human beings, both writers imply,
have two major enemies: their own passions and modern
society. And between the two, you can't win.

The plays of Arthur Miller again reveal the same preoccupation with the individual who is defeated by society
or by his own passions. Miller's major work, *Death of a
Salesman,* is interesting because it is about an organization

man and his defeat. Its enormous success in America was undoubtedly due to the fact that so many Americans felt just like Miller about the organization, about the Protestant ethic of success, about the struggle to keep going and pay off the installments on the washing machine and the car and the mortgage on the house.

The interest is centered on two characters: Willy Loman, the worn-out salesman who has devoted his life to the organization and the American success legend, and is now tired, perpetually nagged by money worries, and on the point of being cold-bloodedly fired by the organization; and his son, Biff, a Beat Generation character who doesn't know what he wants out of life or how to get it, the "crazy mixed-up kid" who has been completely taken in by his father's talk about material success and who now drifts from job to job, hopelessly lost.

There is no action in the play. By various expressionistic devices, Miller reveals the complete bankruptcy — financial and spiritual — of this "typical American home." Even so, it is doubtful whether the Great American Public realized that an attack on its way of life was intended. (Miller records hearing one member of the audience leaving the theater with the comment, "I always knew that New England territory was no good.") And the cause of Biff's embitterment, his resentment of his father, is obscured by having him discover Willy in a state of undress with another woman. The fact that it is Willy's hitch-your-wagon-to-a-star philosophy that is responsible for Biff's lostness is overlaid for the sake of a theatrically effective scene.

The play is a gloomy indictment of the Protestant ethic of success, of the idea of society as hero. But Miller's weakness lies in his lack of imaginative vision. He can condemn the Protestant ethic, but he has nothing to put in its place. He can reject the organization, but he has not shown a single example of fruitful individualism. This is even more apparent in his next two plays, *The Crucible* and *A View from the Bridge*. Both these plays, it goes without saying, are about defeat. The villain of *The Crucible* is society; its main theme is the Salem witch trials and, by implication, the McCarthy witch hunt. But the play also deals with one of Miller's more dubious themes, the need for atonement for sin (or, rather, for wrongdoing, for I doubt whether Miller would like to be thought religious). Proctor, the "hero" of the play (insofar as it has a hero — Miller is more interested in its villains), has gone to bed with Abigail, the girl who starts the witch hunt. So when, at the end of the play, he prefers to be hanged rather than to sign a confession that will save his life, he goes to the scaffold feeling that he has atoned for his sin. (This theme of atonement occurs in an earlier play, *All My Sons,* where its relevance seems just as dubious — although it certainly makes for "good theater.")

A View from the Bridge has for its central character a sort of later version of the Hairy Ape. Eddie Carbone is a longshoreman who seems to be partly in love with his niece, Catherine. When she falls in love with Rodolpho, an illegal Italian immigrant, he becomes increasingly jealous, and when he knows she has had sexual relations with Rodolpho, his jealousy rises to a frenzy. He then betrays Rodolpho to the immigration authorities. But Catherine determines to marry Rodolpho: if she does so, he will be able to remain in America. In a final outburst, Eddie attacks Rodolpho's brother with a knife and is stabbed himself. The play seems curiously pointless. One

THE EVIDENCE OF LITERATURE

is left uncertain as to which forces have destroyed Eddie, or what it all amounts to anyway, except as another demonstration of a man's defeat.

But in the preface to his plays, Miller has at least one remark that goes to the core of the problem:

> Not only in the drama, but in sociology, psychiatry and religion, the past half-century has created an almost overwhelming documentation of man as a nearly passive creation of environment. . . . If only from the dramatic point of view, this dictum cannot be accepted as final. . . . It is no more "real," however, for drama to "liberate" itself from this vice by the route of romance and the spectacle of free will and a new heroic formula than it is "real" now to represent man's defeat as the ultimate implication of an overwhelming determinism.

This may be true, but Miller gives the impression that he belongs to the defeat tradition.

For a writer who is regarded in America as an intellectual (or an "egghead," as *Time* magazine called him), there is very little intellectual fiber in his plays. He emerges as an emotionalist, making his emotional protest against the Protestant ethic in *Death of a Salesman* and since then adding very little that is constructive to that protest. If his ultimate aim is to show men who are not "passive creations of environment," he cannot claim to have accomplished it yet. Insofar as his characters react against environment, it is an emotional rebellion that has no more intellectual content than the revolt of James Dean or the "Beats." When Miller spoke of "romance and the spectacle of free will and a new heroic formula," he was probably thinking of a return of the old Drury Lane melodramas in a modern setting, something on an altogether less serious level than his own work. But one wonders whether Miller has thought carefully about the possibility of creating a more positive character of revolt than Willy or Biff Loman. As a symptom of free will and revolt, *The Organization Man* is more heartening than *Death of a Salesman;* certainly more constructive and analytical. Here, perhaps, is the direction that Miller has missed since *Death of a Salesman.*

But if Miller has failed so far to create an inner-directed man, he is at least conscious of the necessity. He has started to break away from the tradition of man totally dominated by society or his own weaknesses. Elmer Rice had been the first American dramatist to catch this tone of total defeat, in his expressionistic fantasy, *The Adding Machine,* a sort of dramatized *1984* about a clerk who has worked for the same firm for twenty-five years and is now about to be replaced by an adding machine. At the end of the play, Mr. Zero (now in heaven) learns that he must return to earth for many more incarnations, and is destined to end as a slave working a super-adding machine in a coal mine. Rice's later play, *Street Scene,* is about a New York tenement; its bewildered characters, in Miller's phrase, are more helpless reflections of their environment. The basic assumptions of Rice — bewilderment and defeat — are the main themes of O'Neill and Williams. Even if Miller's revolt is emotional and unconstructive, as it has been to date, the revolt in itself suggests that the Rice formula is out of date and that the time has arrived to consider some new hypothesis.

When one surveys the total field of modern American writing, one sees to what extent the hero has become a passive figure. It is as if the Protestant ethic had drained literature of all vitality, of everything but an exhausted realism. As expounded by the American businessman, the Protestant ethic had emphasized the need for a man to better himself, to display energy and vitality; but the "bettering" was purely material, the vitality was to be directed solely towards money-making. No writer can work upon such assumptions; if he swallows them consciously, they will produce a state of emotional indigestion.

This is perhaps what happened to American writing; Sinclair Lewis's satire on the American businessman, *Babbitt*, was no bitter condemnation; Babbitt is a bumbling, pottering, American Mr. Polly, and rather lovable. Dreiser's *An American Tragedy* shows the defeat of a man who has accepted the Protestant ethic, but Clyde Griffiths ends in the death cell as a victim of fate (in the Hardy manner) rather than as a dupe of the go-getter ethic.

One other American writer, who could hardly be ignored in a survey of contemporary writing, I have left until this point because, to some extent, his work stands outside these trends. Hemingway's cosmopolitanism seems to have saved him from the tone of utter defeat that pervades the work of most contemporary American writers. Because his subjects are the Canadian backwoods, the bull rings of Spain, fishing in Florida, hunting in Africa, he can command a more vital, individualistic tone than most of his contemporaries and his younger American imitators. And he is interesting because he undoubtedly feels the need for a more heroic, individualistic tone. After the stunted heroes of Dos Passos, Anderson, Lewis, Sinclair, and the others, it is a relief to turn to *The Sun Also Rises* or *A Farewell to Arms* and to find men who are still enthusiastic about fine mornings, good wine, sex, sport, and being alive. Yet, as the years have gone by, Hemingway has shown himself to be a child of his time. In the early books there was a feeling of active revolt against the unheroic premise of his contemporaries (he wrote a satire on Anderson). In *A Farewell to Arms,* in the scene with the ants on the burning log, he gloomily concludes that it is impossible to win against life: "You died. You did not know what it was all about. You never had time to learn. . . . Stay around and they would kill you." It is almost as if this was Hemingway's acknowledgment of defeat. After *A Farewell to Arms,* sensitivity seems to have disappeared from his work. *Green Hills of Africa* retains the optimism and refusal to be defeated, at the cost of complete insensitivity. It is a retreat from the complexity of life, a literary back-to-nature act. This is also true of his much-praised story *The Old Man and the Sea,* which seems to me to be a highly suspect work of fake simplicity, from which all his earlier virtues have been subtracted — the contemporary relevance, the sense of moral bewilderment. The individualism, the heroism, has hardened into a sort of dramatic gesture, which made one critic, reviewing *To Have and Have Not,* complain that she wished Mr. Hemingway would come out from behind the hair on his chest. Hemingway's achievement and influence are undeniable, but to his younger imitators he must seem a walking declaration that defeat is unavoidable.

Some of these younger imitators are studied in Edmund Wilson's excellent essay, "The Boys in the Back Room" (in *Classics and Commercials*). He writes of James M. Cain, John O'Hara, William Saroyan, Hans Otto Storm, and John Steinbeck. As Mr. Wilson points out, the cultural foundations of these writers are altogether narrower than those of the older generation. Reading their work tends to produce a slightly stifled feeling. They add to the Hemingway sense of defeat a feeling of writing in a narrow room (hence, perhaps, Mr. Wilson's title). There is no deep sense of Nature (as in Hemingway), and no sense whatever of man as an evolving spiritual being. Society comes first and last. Their work is all of people: people are its limit and its horizon.

Then there is the Beat Generation. For English readers, its best-known representatives are the novelist Jack Kerouac and the poet Allen Ginsberg. There can be no possible doubt that they represent a kind of revolt; but it is difficult to discover a great deal more. Kerouac's novel, *On the Road,* is dedicated to the sense of speed. It is told by a narrator who hitchhikes around the country, drinks too much, listens to jazz, tries to seduce girls (unsuccessfully), returns to his home town, and prepares to start all over again. It would seem to be the other side of the coin from Riesman's Found Generation, a complete rejection of security. In an article in the *Chicago Review,* Kerouac says: "The new American poetry as typified by the San Francisco Renaissance (which means Ginsberg, me, Rexroth, Ferlinghetti, McClure, Corso, Gary Snyder, Phil Lamantia, Philip Whalen, I guess) is a kind of new-old Zen lunacy poetry, writing whatever comes into your head." After expounding his principle for half a page, Kerouac refers caustically to Eliot and "his dreary negative rules like the objective correlative, etc., which is just a lot of constipation." Zen is often mentioned by these writers; apparently it symbolizes for them pure instinct, a revolt against intellect and the "higher criticism" that the Americans have shown such skill in developing over the past twenty years.

The San Francisco school achieves vigor at the expense of content. Kerouac has further expounded his anti-classic principle in the *Evergreen Review*, in a piece called "Essentials of Spontaneous Prose," which ends: "If possible, write 'without consciousness' in semi-trance." He uses sexual symbolism, speaks of writing as an "orgasm," and says, "*Come* from within." T. E. Hulme has expressed the objection to this in a single clear image: "The bird attained whatever grace its shape possesses not as a result of the mere desire for flight, but because it had to fly *in air, against gravitation.*" In view of the freshness that the San Francisco school have brought to their writing, it seems a pity to beat them over the head with Hulme. But because their writing *does* seem to be a revolt, a pure reflex action against other-direction, it is difficult to feel much faith in its outcome. The successful revolutionist takes care to appear constitutional.

American literature in the twentieth century, then, supports the analyses of Riesman and Whyte. It shows two main tendencies, which could be labeled Society as Hero and Society as Villain. In either case, the individual is reduced to a cipher to be defeated and crushed, or to fit in quietly and place his virtues at the service of the organization, like Prewett in *From Here to Eternity*. There would seem to be no third way.

The English Scene

J. B. Priestley's *Thoughts in the Wilderness*, which I have already mentioned, might be regarded as raw material for a sociological study of contemporary England along the same lines as *The Lonely Crowd*. The salient point that emerges is that modern English society is more other-directed than a good Englishman might like to think.

In England, as in America, the character of the younger generation is formed mainly by television and the cinema. When the rock-'n'-roll film *Rock Around the Clock* came to England in 1956, there were scenes of rowdyism in cinemas all over the country. Teen-agers jived in the aisles or on the stage and started fights when they were interrupted. (Similar scenes were reported from Germany.) The youth of England also showed itself in no way behind the youth of America in the hysteria with which it greeted visiting crooners, from Frank Sinatra to Johnny Ray. And local watch committees have made it clear that they believe that films depicting juvenile delinquency have an influence on teen-age audiences; Marlon Brando's film *The Wild Ones* has been almost universally banned in the British Isles. (I have already quoted Harrison Salisbury on the influence of such films on American teen-agers.)

The tendency to cater to the other-direction of adult audiences has been seen over the past ten years or so in such popular radio and TV programs as *Mrs. Dale's Diary, The Archers, Starr and Company.* Such programs are concerned with ordinary people, and their level of interest is usually about that of a *Girl's Crystal* serial story. It is true, of course, that there has been a magazine market for this type of material for the past thirty years; but the audience reached by radio or television is immensely wider than that reached by *Woman's Own.* It is hardly necessary to point out the contrast with the popular literature of a century or more ago, in which the female reader was invited to identify herself with the heroine and to imagine herself in situations that required some degree of inner-

direction. From Richardson's *Pamela* and *Clarissa* down
through Byron's heroines to the women of Victorian melo-
drama, the female reader was persuaded to imagine herself in extraordinary situations from which she could
extricate herself only by strength of character. And perhaps the classic example is that favorite heroine of the
silent film, the girl who, though tied to the railway line,
still refused to surrender her maidenhood to the villain.
This, of course, might be a mixed blessing (as Joyce's portrait of Gerty Macdowell in *Ulysses* showed), but it undoubtedly encouraged a sense of idealism, of standards of
conduct that are outside the personal interests of the
reader. The *Mrs. Dale's Diary* type of entertainment derives its popularity from a sort of flattery of its audience.
"You may be ordinary, but you're better off that way."
The everyday life of the audience is taken as the norm.
The good characters are socially well-adjusted; the bad
ones tend to be curmudgeons or are obviously self-centered.
The conflicts portrayed are those of ordinary life, on a level
of conscientious triviality. And yet the technique differs
from that of the folk drama of the past in having no particular center of gravity; plays like *Gammer Gurton's
Needle* and *Master Pathelin* were uninhibited farces, while
the *Yorkshire Tragedy* used its material in the manner of
a modern thriller. The *Mrs. Dale's Diary* type of serial
takes care to fall into no category; its aim is to impress its
audience as ordinary life.

This is typical of England in the mid-twentieth century,
and it is, perhaps, an English equivalent of the *Main Street*
and *Ten North Frederick* trend in the United States. It is
a sign of the all-dominating cult of the "ordinary chap"
that has for many years pervaded English, as well as Ameri-

can, literature. Mr. Priestley has said of the young English novelists that as a rule their central characters are too deliberately unheroic. But the trend he is observing has been developing for several decades, and he himself has contributed something to it. (His family in *Laburnam Grove* are close relations of the Archers and the Dales.)

In England in the 1950's, there has been a certain movement of revolt among serious writers. Some critics have therefore felt that things may not be so bad after all. (Throughout the 1940's, it was a critical commonplace to say that the novel was at an end, and some critics even expressed a fear that the work of the Joyce-Eliot generation had made it impossible for literature to go any further.) It is interesting to examine some of these new writers by the standards of Riesman and Whyte, and to see how far their revolt is actually a new direction.

One of the first writers to attract attention in the 1950's was Angus Wilson. His first two volumes of short stories were notable for the intense dislike with which he seemed to regard all his characters; his attitude was not unlike that of Aldous Huxley in *Point Counter Point*. Yet in spite of the wit and trenchancy of the satire, the whole approach bore strong resemblances to the *Mrs. Dale's Diary* type of entertainment. The stories were all about "ordinary people," and the characters were, almost without exception, other-directed; they were either nice or not nice (mostly the latter). But it is perhaps hardly fair to observe the other-directed tendency of these early volumes, since satire is, by its very nature, about other-directed people. All its emphasis is on motives, on the weakness and contemptibleness of its characters. But Mr. Wilson's later work has shown that he is not to be considered as a satirist; there are many of his characters whom he seems to like and to take quite seriously. Even so, they remain essentially socially oriented; their problems are all to do with other people. The effect is occasionally that of a highbrow *Woman's Own* serial. The preoccupation with other people is declared immediately in the first sentence of his latest novel, *The Middle Age of Mrs. Eliot.* "Meg Eliot was well aware that in taking her place as the Chairman of the Committee for the third time in succession, she was acting in an unconstitutional way." And later, on the same page: "Meg felt a bit ashamed when she considered how she had persuaded them." Similarly, the dilemmas of his central characters are always connected with their relations to other people; the hero of *Hemlock and After,* the writer Bernard Sands, is a humanist whose inner complacency is shattered by two things: his development of homosexual tendencies in middle age, and his observation that he feels a sadistic pleasure on seeing a male prostitute arrested in Leicester Square. It is not his salvation he is worried about (like the heroes of Sartre and Camus), but the fact that his relation to society is not what he thought it was; the discovery of his real relation to it gives him a sense of guilt that leads to his death. In *Anglo-Saxon Attitudes,* the central character is a historian whose personal life has been highly unsatisfactory — mostly owing to his moral cowardice — and who suspects that a historical discovery in which he took part is actually a fraud. At the end of the book, he manages to straighten out his personal relations to some extent and announces to the historical world that the discovery was a fraud, thus propitiating society. His inner life now runs smoothly because his personal relations have been established on a more satisfactory basis and his relation to society has been adjusted. He can now go off for a holiday to Mexico with a light heart.

This survey of his work certainly fails to do justice to Mr. Wilson's skill as a manipulator of scores of characters, as well as to his extraordinary powers of observation. Nevertheless, none of these characters can be considered as inner-directed in the sense that the great inner-directed characters of literature can be — Faust, or Ahab in *Moby Dick*, or even Prewett in *From Here to Eternity*. Mr. Wilson's characters bring to mind that passage at the beginning of Shaw's *Apple Cart* in which Sempronius talks about his father, who had spent his life arranging pageants and who, when he was cast up alone on a desert island, went melancholy-mad from solitude. Mr. Wilson's characters also exist solely as social entities. All their thoughts are occupied with other people. Perhaps Mr. Wilson's tendency to call them all by their Christian names emphasizes the *Mrs. Dale's Diary* affinities; but it is something deeper than these odd literary tricks that gives his work its tone of other-direction. The very seriousness of his intentions underlines the fact that society is for him what the Church might have been for a writer in the Middle Ages; it occupies the whole of his horizon, and he shows no interest in what lies beyond it.

Although Mr. Wilson published his first volume in 1949, he actually belongs to an older generation of writers; he is now in his mid-forties. The most notorious literary revolt of the fifties is associated with the names of a younger set of writers, whose ages range from twenty to thirty-five. The first thing to note about most of them — the best known are Kingsley Amis, John Wain, John Braine, John Osborne, Bill Hopkins, Michael Hastings, Stuart Holroyd

— is a certain bluntness in their language and a down-to-earth quality in their attitudes. It is the opposite of the high-flown quality that De Tocqueville noted in American orators. It seems to be a determination not to say anything they don't feel. But the question that will determine their importance is, what *do* they feel? And this is altogether less definite. They have been lumped together as Angry Young Men, but the phrase is almost completely irrelevant; they are no more or less angry than any previous generation of writers.

John Wain set the tone of revolt in his *Hurry On Down*. This novel deals with a young man who leaves university with the right qualifications for becoming a schoolteacher or for getting some minor executive post in industry. But he has no desire to settle down, and prefers to drift from job to job — as a window cleaner, a TV script writer, and so on. There is no conclusion (except a rather dubious ending that involves "the love of a good woman" — a device that Nietzsche exploded when he wrote of Wagner's *Flying Dutchman*). The point of the novel is its hero's desire to be inner-directed instead of "fitting in." But its revolt is as inconclusive as that of the Beat Generation.

The same criticisms can be made of Amis's *Lucky Jim*. Again, the main point about Jim is his refusal to fit in. He is a university lecturer who dislikes a great many things about his job but hasn't the courage to revolt openly. The humor of the book arises from the contrast between the violence of his thoughts and the submissiveness of his actions. In many respects, Jim has the characteristics of the typical Aldous Huxley hero — the ability to put his foot in it, to make a mess of things, a sort of wincing sensi-

tivity about his *faux pas*. But the book's popularity arises
from quite a different source: from the fact that, in spite
of his *faux pas*, Jim still gets the girl and lands the important job. The reader who sympathizes only too painfully with Jim's sense of ordinariness is delighted to be
assured that he has nothing to be ashamed of, that the
ordinary chap will always come out on top. Together,
Amis and Wain launched a new cult of the ordinary chap,
who is only Riesman's other-directed man with a veneer
of rebelliousness.

The revolt of John Osborne has the same dubious quality. His first successful play, *Look Back in Anger,* gave
the impression that a new revolt against society had hit
the British theater. It was true that the hero's revolt had
a strong pessimistic flavor — "There aren't any good, brave
causes left" — but at least it was alive and kicking, it
wasn't fatalistic. But Mr. Osborne's next play, *The Entertainer,* written after his fabulous success, is as pessimistic
as *The Iceman Cometh.* It concerns a number of theatrical
people in a seaside boardinghouse who get on each other's
nerves for three acts. Nothing happens, except that everything goes from bad to worse and that its hero, the third-
rate comedian Archie Rice, shows a disinclination to "make
a fresh start" in Canada, preferring to go to jail. It looks
like masochism, or exhausted defeatism, although Mr.
Osborne tries hard to make it look like a sort of integrity.
Since *The Entertainer,* an earlier play of Mr. Osborne's
has been shown in London, in which he is again preoccupied with the autobiographical-type hero who has a griev-
ance against society. The hero of *Epitaph for George
Dillon* has the same capacity for invective and self-pity

as Jimmy Porter in *Look Back in Anger,* but the play shows him abandoning his integrity and writing cheap melo-dramas for provincial touring companies.

The revolt of Amis, Wain, and Osborne lacks direction. It tends to be a wild thrashing around that demonstrates nothing but dissatisfaction. Moreover, their involvement in the cult of the ordinary chap shows that they are very far from extricating themselves from the premises they believe they are attacking.

John Braine, in *Room at the Top,* is far more in con-trol of his material than are Amis, Wain, or Osborne. He boldly returns to a major theme of the nineteenth century — the need to assert oneself in society, to become a man of importance — a theme to be found in Balzac, Zola, Stendhal. In this respect, he has already thrown off the defeat premise that dominates the American scene. But it must not be supposed that he set out deliberately to return to an earlier tradition. Joe Lampton's aspirations are not merely to make money, to achieve power; his ambitious-ness is as thoroughly romantic as Jay Gatsby's in Fitzgerald's novel. The injustice of his own dull life as an office worker hits him for the first time as he watches a beautiful, sun-burned girl climb into a Jaguar with a well-dressed youth. His is a completely romantic fantasy, a longing for every-thing that he imagines the girl and the Jaguar symbolize.

All the same, the novel is not about Joe's struggle for money. After stating his theme, Braine seems to forget it, and goes on to describe Joe's experiences with the local dramatic society and the two love affairs he gets involved in. These two affairs become the center of the novel — one with a teen-age girl, the other with an older woman (as in Stendhal's *Le Rouge et le Noir*). At the end of the novel, he jilts the older woman and marries the teen-age girl, whose father is a rich factory owner and can offer Joe a well-paid job. The older woman kills herself in a car crash, and Joe is left suffering from pangs of conscience and a feeling of emptiness — in spite of the fact that he is now a prosperous man with an attractive wife. The moral overtones are unmistakable.

It would be a complete misinterpretation of the book to regard Joe as a social climber with a one-track mind. Passages like this contradict the idea:

> Then I thought of Sparrow Hill and Warley Moor again. I knew that there was a cold wind outside and a light covering of snow. It would be quiet there and untouched and clean. The beer went dead inside me; I felt with my own selfishness, as nasty as catarrh; there was nothing in my heart to match the lovely sweep of the moor and the sense of infinite space behind it and a million extra stars above.

Moreover, the death of Alice focuses the unresolved problem of human suffering and the necessity for indifference. (In *Les Faux Monnayeurs*, Lillian persuades Vincent to abandon his mistress by telling him of a shipwreck in which she was involved; the boat was loaded to capacity, and the sailors hacked off the fingers of those who tried to climb into it with hatchets — one more passenger would have sunk the boat. Gide here expresses the problem with great power.) It is not that Joe *wants* to abandon Alice; but he has to make the choice that involves all his dreams of riches.

The important thing about this novel is that it is a revival of the inner-directed hero. Most criticisms of it that I have read suggest that Joe is an unsympathetic, grasping character, but nothing could be further from the truth; the author has obviously poured a great deal of his own longing and imagining into him — and above all, of his own sensitivity (for Joe is by no means insensitive). The total effect is of a tone very like *A Farewell to Arms* — the love of life, the mixture of sensitivity and toughness in the hero, and the same final sense of tragedy and loss. It was startling that a book of such extraordinary merit should have been written, not by a widely traveled journalist, but by a Yorkshire librarian.

Bill Hopkins's *The Divine and the Decay* has many of the same qualities as Braine's book, although technically it is a far less satisfying job. Its hero, Peter Plowart, has a bottomless contempt for most human beings, which seems to be based on the same kind of observations as those of Riesman and Whyte. But Plowart's situation is made more interesting by the fact that he himself is by no means inner-directed; he is always being seized by misgivings and self-doubt. His whole attitude towards the world is based on his certainty that he is not like other men, and he wants to prove this to himself by gaining political powers, by becoming the second Napoleon. But he is self-divided: certain of his own superiority and the stupidity of most men; yet, as soon as he is left alone, torn by the realization that he has not yet achieved self-control. The plot of the book is too complex to be detailed here, and frequently fails to convince. But the inner situation of its hero is always convincing; and the climax of the book, when Plowart's self-division is healed in a moment of crisis, has considerable power. But the book stops at the very moment when the reader wants to know what happens next, the moment when the author is challenged to show what his hero will *do* now that he is no longer self-divided. Although Hopkins makes a far more determined attempt to explore the problems of the inner-directed man than Osborne or Amis, he still leaves most of the questions unanswered.

The situation in England is, on the whole, more promising than in America. This may be for exactly the reasons that Whitehead suggested made the English student more self-determined and confident than the American: the English writer has a lack of diffidence, a willingness to tear into problems without too much fear of making a fool of himself. This usually means that English writing tends to be less technically polished than American (no English novel of the fifties can compare, for sheer technical skill, with Grace Metalious's *Peyton Place*). But it also means that there is a stronger sense of individualism. By its very nature, individualism is a revolt against other-direction. But unless it possesses a sense of conscious purpose, the revolt is likely to express itself as a futile gesture of protest. This is the major complaint to be brought against writers like Amis, Wain, and Osborne. They seem to lack an awareness of the central problems, or to be aware only of their nonessential aspects. These problems are fundamentally psychological. They spring from the fact that the complexity of our society tends to create a defensive attitude in many people, the sort of acknowledgment of defeat that a schoolboy might feel on looking into a volume of higher mathematics. The result is a sense of diffidence, a loss of the feeling of being self-determined. This diffidence gnaws into the nervous energies, into the power of enterprise; it narrows the individual's conception of his own abilities and values.

The Lonely Crowd and *The Organization Man* examine this attitude in its sociological aspects, treating its literary manifestations merely as evidence. But neither Riesman nor Whyte deals with the most important symptoms in contemporary literature, *the diminishing role of the hero, and the cult of the ordinary chap.* This is the matter of greatest concern for the contemporary writer.

The first signs of this new anti-heroic consciousness began to reveal themselves in the 1920's, in the work of such men as Eliot, Joyce, Huxley. After the generation of Shaw, Chesterton, Wells, who regarded themselves as all-rounders, capable of pronouncing on politics, religion, literature, culture, even sport, came a generation who deliberately narrowed their approach. Eliot said, typically, "The spirit killeth, but the letter giveth life." Joyce excluded any general ideas from his work and seemed to think of himself as closer to the painter or musician, a "pure artist," rather than a writer. Pound declared his admiration for Flaubert and James. Huxley stuck to a cultured satire, and only in later years began to state — somewhat diffidently — his positive values.* It is true that this revolt began as a repudiation of the carelessness and irresponsibility that so often reveal themselves in the work of the Shaw-Chesterton generation, but caution and understatement soon developed into an unwritten law, which strengthened the diffidence premise, whose social causes Riesman has analyzed.

---

* The diffidence has never left his work, and appears as a definite weakness premise in all his novels. I have dealt with this theme at length in the *London Magazine*, August, 1958.

The result has been a quarter of a century of increasingly diluted imitation of the "great names" of the twenties.

The present generation is consequently in a cleft stick. It is hardly surprising that critics after the war began to declare that literature had reached a point of exhaustion and that no great names were likely to arise in our epoch. Good writing is usually a reflection of and a reaction against its time. The work of Shaw and Wells cannot be understood without knowing that they grew up in late-Victorian England. The work of Eliot, Huxley, Joyce, and Hemingway is post-war; the 1914-1918 war always lurks in the background. But the powerful forces of our own age are mass media. Shaw could react directly against Victorian prudery, and Eliot could react against post-Victorian complacency (which included Shaw and Wells). The modern writer has nothing so well-defined to start from. Among other things, he has to react against *Mrs. Dale's Diary*, Diana Dors, American success worship and British royalty worship, the *News of the World* and the *New Statesman*, T. S. Eliot and Dale Carnegie and *Forever Amber*, the hydrogen bomb, James Dean, the Jehovah's Witnesses, and Wilfred Pickles. If he is born into a working-class or lower-middle-class family, all these things will be woven into the fabric of his life from an early age or will obtrude themselves into it as he starts to take an interest in the world outside. And even if a young writer made the effort to get all these things in focus, he would still have solved only a half of his problems. Shaw could begin writing where Dickens and Carlyle left off, and Eliot could turn his back on Shaw and plump for Newman and T. E. Hulme. But the writer of today finds that the Eliot-Joyce-Hemingway tradition of writing has now worked itself to a dead halt, and he will have

difficulty in feeling himself a part of a tradition. He is
faced with difficult alternatives. He could write as if Shaw,
Wells, Eliot, Joyce, and the rest had never existed. (This
seems to be what Mr. Amis has done.) In that case, he is
bound to take himself fairly lightly. Or he could attempt
to synthesize within himself the whole movement of writing
in the twentieth century, attempting to act as arbitrator
between Shaw and Eliot, Greene and Chesterton, D. H.
Lawrence and Wells, and to base his own work on a total
reassessment of the past sixty years. In doing this, he would
also be working against the modern trend of other-direction, which makes him feel that to undertake such a task
would be an absurd overestimate of his own powers and
importance. The decision to attempt it would be the most
important step.

If the bewildering variety of revolt in the fifties can be
said to demonstrate any single point, it would be this —
that revolt for its own sake is not enough. It fails to get
to the core of the problem: the increasing other-direction
in modern society and the disappearance of the hero, the
inner-directed man, in literature. This is the problem that
has to be brought into sharp, conscious focus.

Conclusion

So far in this essay, I have stayed close to the method of
analysis used by Riesman and Whyte. I have tried to show
the extent to which other-direction has become such a basic
attitude in modern culture that it affects all our thinking.
It has reached such a point that one might almost say that
there are only two kinds of writer today: the ones who take
other-direction for granted and the ones who feel some

intuitive revolt against it. Such a generalization, of course, would not be strictly accurate. Nevertheless, it may be regarded as a useful simplification of the argument, one that makes the issues quite clear.

Whyte and Riesman devote very little space to literature, and what they do quote is intended to illustrate other-direction on the simplest level. In the present section, I have tried to show that there are types of other-direction that are highly deceptive. They appear as revolt for its own sake, and the casual observer might be inclined to mistake them for inner-direction. In fact, they are no more inner-direction than is the action of a snake in strik-ing at a moving object. Their reflex nature is proved by their lack of direction, their failure to think beyond the actual gesture of defiance, and the speed with which their revolt subsides when the gesture meets with success. The writer who finds that his revolt commands a flattering at-tention quickly assumes the characteristics of other-direc-tion, accepting its standards and values, and demonstrates his fundamental lack of concern with questions of value. There is no attempt to think beyond the revolt, since the revolt itself was never more than an emotional reaction. When the smoke clears and the shouting dies down, it becomes apparent that it was only an appearance of revolt disguising the old defeatism and fatigue.

But the method of Riesman and Whyte, by its very nature, leaves the task half finished. Their criticism is essentially negative; starting from their premises, this is unavoidable. Inner-direction is undoubtedly a value of the utmost importance, but it is not the simple thing that Riesman makes it appear. It is a term that covers a thou-sand psychological problems. Without a more precise at-

tempt at analysis of these problems, it is impossible to
progress beyond the conclusions of *The Lonely Crowd,* its
vague hope that the other-directed will experience a change
of heart.

Riesman speaks as if the change from inner-direction to
other-direction first began to make itself apparent in the
twentieth century, as a direct result of economic pressures.
But the truth is far more complex. The increase of other-
direction is not merely a matter of the increase of big business, advertising, mass production, and so on. It has also
been helped by the fact that the cultural forces of inner-
direction have been self-divided for a very long time now;
its enemies are internal as well as external. Until these
internal problems have been solved, there can be no hope
for an effective rebellion against other-direction. The next
section of this essay will be devoted to an attempt to express the nature of these problems.

IF ECONOMY
IS NOT
CHANGED
ANYTHING
ELSE IS
NOTHING
BUT HOPELESS

Part Three

The Anatomy
of Insignificance

I glory in the name of earwig.

GUMBRIL, IN ALDOUS HUXLEY'S *Antic Hay*

With people who know how to revenge themselves, and to stand up for themselves in general — how is it done? Why, when they are possessed . . . by a feeling of revenge, then for the time being, there is nothing but that feeling left in their whole being. Such a gentleman simply dashes straight for his object, like an infuriated bull, with its horns down, and nothing but a wall will stop him. . . . Well, such a direct person I regard as the real, normal man. . . . I envy such a man till I am green in the face. He is stupid. I am not disputing that, but perhaps the normal man should be stupid. And I am more persuaded of that suspicion . . . by the fact that, if you take the antithesis of the normal man, that is, the man of acute consciousness, he genuinely thinks of himself as a mouse, not as a man.

DOSTOEVSKY: *Notes from Underground*

WHEN Dostoevsky wrote the passage quoted above, he put his finger on the center of the problem that obstructs the twentieth-century writer from creating a great heroic figure. Heroism is not mere physical courage and conviction. If a man sailed a rubber dinghy up the Congo and then dived in among the crocodiles, armed with nothing but a toasting fork, we would not call him a hero; we should more likely call him a fool. If a man went over Niagara Falls in a barrel, we might admire his rash courage, but we would think of him as a gambler rather than as a hero. Heroism is not merely courage; it is *directed* courage; and what it is directed towards is all important. Probably many of Al Capone's gangsters possessed qualities that would have made them excellent warriors under Attila the Hun; but in twentieth-century Chicago, they were dangerous and undesirable. The qualities that make the hero depend upon the time he lives in.

This suggests a generalization about the hero: he is the man who, in some way, embodies the qualities most needed by his age. The religious passion and the ruthlessness of King David would have been out of place in ancient Greece; the cunning of Ulysses would have been an undesirable virtue in the age of Malory's King Arthur; the blind reliance on fate of Sinbad the Sailor would not have ensured his survival in the Israel of 1000 B.C. These men have one thing in common: they are "favorites of the gods" (or of God). But as heroes, they are tied to a particular period in history.

What are the qualities required by the hero in the twentieth century? To answer this question would be a major step towards answering the problems posed by Riesman and Whyte. It is obvious, without further investigation, that our age is a great deal more complex than any previous period in history; a hero who possesses simple courage, or faith without intelligence, would be a failure. The hero of the twentieth century would need to be something of a metaphysician.

An important preliminary step would be to understand the cultural developments that have made the old hero inadequate. They can be traced in the literature of the past three centuries. The figure of the hero in literature reflects the needs of the age and the degree to which men of each age have overcome their problems. What Eliot called "a sense of one's own age" is also a sense of the problems of one's age; certain artists may achieve an embodiment of these problems in their work. Hamlet, Faust, Ahab, Zarathustra, the Underground Man reach this symbolic stature; our own century can offer no comparable symbols. The reason for this failure can be better understood through an analysis of these symbolic figures of the past. It will be seen that the reasons for the disappearance of the hero figure go deeper than a shift from an age of production to an age of consumption; they are bound up with the inner dynamics of the hero. The present section is mainly concerned with a definition of these internal problems.

What Is a Hero?

First, it would be valuable to have a provisional definition of the word "hero." This is not as difficult as may at
first appear. All that is necessary is to get a clear mental
picture of the man who is *not* heroic. I am not thinking
of the coward, but of the man who is completely contented
in his way of life — or if not contented, at least too lazy and
half-alive to do anything about it. The idea of a hero is
of a man who needs to *expand,* who needs wider fields for
his activities. He is the man who cannot accept the status
quo. He is the man for whom the idea of freedom is a
contradiction of his present way of life. The anti-hero is
the man who accepts, who "fits in."

It will remain true, of course, that the hero's capacity
for heroism will depend on how concrete are his ideas of
freedom. If his country is under enemy rule, and his idea
of freedom means political freedom, then his heroism will
have free play until his country is once again self-governed.
On the other hand, one could imagine a bank clerk who
possesses the latent military genius of a Napoleon but who
has never become aware of it. Unless a war happens to
place him in a position of military command, he will probably remain a dissatisfied bank clerk. He may, it is true,
have his imagination stirred by a war film or a book about
the army and decide to change his career. But even so, it
will depend largely upon chance as to whether he ever
becomes a hero.

Heroism, in its purest definition, is an appetite for
freedom, a desire to live more intensely. But its realization depends upon the liveliness of the potential hero's
imagination, upon how far he can understand his own
latent needs and devise an outlet for them. It might very

well have been different in more primitive societies, where any man of spirit became a soldier and had his opportunities presented to him in the course of his normal routine. He would not need imagination. But in a more complex and peaceful society, a man who feels the craving for expansion, for freedom, needs to possess intelligence and some degree of self-knowledge. And somehow, the words "intelligence," "self-knowledge," "imagination" are are in opposition to the idea of *simple* heroism.

It is true that there is a strong modern tendency to admire physical courage, and that various types of simple heroism are now pouring money into the pockets of the men who write books about it. The war heroes have been revived; we read about men who crossed the Pacific on a raft, or crossed the Atlantic in a dinghy, or climbed Everest or Nanga Parbat. The tough private detective is in great demand. So is the great surgeon, with his white uniform and scalpel. But somehow, these men seem out of date in the age of the organization and mass production, as irrelevant as those brown daguerreotypes of the early motorcars. The pleasure they give is the pleasure of turning away from the present and imagining an age when they *were* relevant.

The Old Hero and the New

But when did the physical hero start to become outdated? It was a great deal further back than the twentieth century. Even in the days of fervent British imperialism, no one regarded the works of Kipling, Conan Doyle, John Buchan, A. E. W. Mason as great literature. In fact, if one turns as far back as Shakespeare, one sees that while his Henry

the Fifth was a patriotic backward look, his greatest characters are the self-divided men, Hamlet and Lear, or the
solitary, Prospero. Hamlet is an amazing anticipation of
the self-divided man of the nineteenth century, the fore-
runner of Goethe's Faust, Dostoevsky's Underground Man,
and the later heroes of Musil and Sartre. (Whether
Shakespeare intended him as such is another matter.)

While Shakespeare was anticipating a new type of hero,
his contemporary, Cervantes, was ringing the death knell
of the old type. Don Quixote is the "normal man" whom
Dostoevsky's Underground Man spoke of, who "lowers
his head and charges like a bull"; he is not merely the
stupid hero, he is downright insane. But Cervantes was
not concerned with the new hero who would replace the
Galahads and Amadis de Gauls. If the question troubled
him at all, he probably thought of Sancho Panza as the new
hero — the hardheaded realist who knows better than to
go out looking for dragons and giants. Cervantes might
claim to have invented the cult of the ordinary chap; he is
the first of a distinguished line of literary men who would
have no truck with heroes: Quevedo, Lesage, Fielding,
Defoe, Smollett . . . in the Sancho Panzas and Tom
Joneses, there is no craving for freedom; all they want is
a wife, a home, and a bottle of wine.

But when the heroic was revived, nearly two centuries
later, the hero brought back with him all the problems
that are still latent in the work of Shakespeare and Cervantes. Schiller's Karl Moor in *The Robbers* is a typical
example. He broods: "Law has never produced a man of
true grandeur. It is freedom that hatches the colossal and
the extreme." But Karl's idea of organizing his friends into
a robber band and taking to the woods like Robin Hood

is a typical romantic miscalculation; he soon learns that practical anarchy is boring and sordid, and that freedom needs to be closely combined with discipline if it is not to degenerate into drifting. Schiller is obliged to solve the problem by killing him off.

Goethe soon ran into the same problem in his own creative experiments and ended by creating the greatest self-divided hero of all. His career had begun with the creation of Goetz von Berlichingen, a backward look into the heroic past, the freedom-seeker whose ideal of freedom is political. But as soon as Goethe tried to write a contemporary story, the hero became the morbidly over-sensitive young Werther, who ends by committing suicide. It is true that Werther is not a typical hero in that he fails to get the girl; but Goethe himself had no illusions about successful love; he had a habit of withdrawing from his own love affairs before he reached the point of living happily ever after. Werther's tragedy is not sexual frustration, it is the fact that the world and he are at loggerheads; he suspects that his craving for freedom is *incapable* of being satisfied in the world.

After *Werther,* Goethe went on to analyze the peculiar psychological complexities of the "new hero" in Faust. At the beginning of the poem Faust is a well-known scholar, universally respected, regarded with veneration by the local peasantry for his medical skill, still young,* personally attractive. It is evident that, at some earlier time, he has been consumed by idealism, the feeling that knowl-

---

* This is of particular interest. Faust is traditionally represented as an old (or elderly) man. Marlowe's Faustus asks for the return of his youth as the first gift of Mephistopheles. Goethe obviously had no wish to load the dice against his hero: all Faust's despair can then be concentrated on his self-division, his sense of internal defeat.

edge could turn man into a god. The result is, now, not merely disillusionment, but a nihilism that involves the whole universe: a feeling that, if a man could shed all his illusions for a moment, he would not want to live. As far as living is concerned, he feels he has reached a dead end. But as he is about to drink poison, he hears the Easter bells and experiences a rush of *temps perdu*, of memories of his childhood, and an absurd, paradoxical feeling of immortality.

The lesson here would seem to be that his net was not fine enough. He had made a bid to become a god-man by trapping ultimate truth. Truth dissolved, and left him feeling like an insect. But just as he has decided that his desire for immortality was illusion, the Easter bells bring back the living essence of his past and stimulate a consuming desire to *live more*. Faust realizes, in a flash of intuition, that truth is subjectivity; that it is no use looking for it in the outside world; that it is contained within himself, in his memories, in the subconscious power house he carries inside him.

But in the next scene Faust has already forgotten this. When Mephistopheles appears and offers to give him "more ecstasy in an hour than he normally feels in a year," it seems a fair offer. He knows that the pursuit of knowledge can never intensify his desire to live, and hopes to exchange it for "the world of direct experience." From this point onwards, it becomes obvious that he has made a mistake. What is more, it seems likely that Faust's mistake is Goethe's, too. The devil's attempt to show Faust a gay time bores him. The love affair with Gretchen provides some satisfaction, but it is apparent that this also begins to bore him, for by the time that Gretchen knows she is

pregnant Faust has allowed Mephistopheles to drag him
off to a witch's frolic. In the second part of the poem he
has a love affair with Helen of Troy and tries to save himself from a sense of uselessness by becoming a public bene-
factor and draining a swamp.

After the opening scene of Part One, the rest is anticlimax. By this, I do not mean that it is artistically an
anticlimax. But for the reader who has grasped the issues
that were stated in the opening scene, the remainder of
the poem is evasion. *Faust* is an artistic success and a
philosophical failure.

Faust's failure is for reasons that would not have worried
Homer or Sir Thomas Malory for a moment. He feels
"immortal longings" in him, the need to be of more-than-
human stature. When the old hero had such feelings, he
simply went off in search of adventure; or, if his urges
were more subtle, in quest of the Holy Grail. But Goethe
possessed an acuter sense of reality than Homer or Malory,
as well as a more modern insight into self-division. He
could not propel Faust into action, for no action could
resolve his inner tensions. How is he to become a hero?
What could he do, given even the fullest opportunities?

In point of fact, Proust penetrated to the heart of the
matter more unerringly than Goethe, for he seized all the
implications of that inner revelation that Faust experiences
on hearing the Easter bells. He describes the sensation with
great exactitude:

> An exquisite pleasure had invaded my senses. . . . All at
> once, the vicissitudes of life became indifferent to me, its dis-
> asters innocuous, its brevity illusory. . . . I had ceased now
> to feel mediocre, accidental, mortal. [*Swann's Way,* Over-
> ture.]

But Proust's Marcel then begins a careful discipline to recover his past. Faust abandons himself only to Mephistopheles, whom he knows to be stupider than himself. At least, Proust knew there was only one way to turn — inwards. Faust keeps his face determinedly outwards and just involves himself more deeply in his original error, *the failure to realize that truth is subjectivity.*

Spengler referred to the culture of the West as a "Faustian culture" and stated that Faust was the typical hero of the modern world. Faust is the man who is torn between two visions: an internal world, where a new sensitivity and knowledge give strange glimpses of immortality, and an external world, where he is increasingly a misfit. One day he feels himself to be a god; the next, an insect. The poles draw wider apart, and the tension between them becomes greater. Man's dual nature, his "greatness and misery" (to borrow Pascal's phrase), obstructs every attempt to arrive at some clear, simple assessment of his place in the universe. And in the confusion, Faust continues to seek for the answers outside himself, to grope from one solution to another, from magic to love affairs and altruism, never at any stage arriving at peace with himself.

I have suggested that the answer Faust missed lay in subjectivity, in turning inwards. But it must be immediately admitted that this is only half a solution. It is rather as if Whyte had ended *The Organization Man* by advising all employees of big combines to throw up their jobs and retire to cork-lined rooms to spend the rest of their days writing immense autobiographical novels. The problem of the hero goes deeper than this. It is not simply a question of turning inwards, but of coming to terms with the

NOT
SELF-
DIVIDED)
PEACE
BETWEEN
MIND +
PSYCHE

THEN FACING OBJECTS

interior problems *and then turning outwards again.* The old hero was the man who lowered his head and charged like a bull. The new hero is too self-divided for this; he has to learn to heal his self-division. The final hero will be the man who has healed the self-division and is again prepared to fling himself back into the social struggle.

Nothing to Be Done — the Romantic Dilemma

I have tried to suggest why the disappearance of the man of heroic stature cannot be explained away as a social problem. At this point, it might be of interest to study the trend in new heroes in the post-Faustian age, before the cult of the ordinary chap.

While Amis and Osborne side-step the question of their heroes' futures by leaving all their problems suspended in the air, the writers of the nineteenth century were inclined to give an illusion of completeness by killing off the hero. Goethe has Faust carried off to heaven by angels who sing that "so long as man strives, he is not beyond redemption." But later writers left the heavenly chorus to the imagination. Schiller's Karl Moor has to die; there is no other way of rounding off the tragedy. Shelley's Alastor is an idealistic young man who is embraced in a dream by a beautiful girl (who probably symbolizes truth or beauty) and wanders from country to country in search of her until he dies. The symbolism is not as absurd as it sounds; it implies clearly that the man who has seen this vision cannot *do* anything to recover it. He can only wander aimlessly, knowing the search is futile, for the vision came internally and he is looking externally. One is reminded of the tramps in Beckett's *Waiting for Godot*

with their periodic complaint: "Nothing to be done."
The Byronic hero, who is sensitive, handsome, and sinful,
usually finds plenty to do (especially by way of sinning)
but has to die in the end because nothing he ever does
makes him feel better. (*Manfred* is a candid imitation of
Faust.) The romantic heroes of Hoffmann, Tieck, Novalis,
and Jean Paul follow the same pattern. In Theodor
Storm's popular *Immensee*, the hero fails to get the girl
and drifts on into old age, sentimentally mooning about
his youth and lost love. As a device for ending the story,
this was even neater than killing off the hero, for it could
give a sense of inevitability, which the arbitrary death of
the hero often lacked, and could distract attention from
the hero's indecision in letting the heroine get away.

But nineteenth-century romanticism, for all its senti-
mentality, had certain advantages over the realism of the
twentieth century. It never lost sight of the importance
of the individual or of the importance of the ideal. The
intensity that is only rarely achieved in twentieth-century
writing, in such books as *From Here to Eternity* or *The
Caine Mutiny*, is achieved every time by the romantic
writers, simply because they were more concerned about
the solitary individual and his relation to nature. As soon
as the reader opens a book by Hoffmann or Kleist or
Brentano, he is transported into a world of greater intensity. The romantics felt no guilty conscience when they
turned their back on society.

Some Nineteenth-Century Heroes

Stendhal's *Le Rouge et le Noir* is of particular interest as
a bridge between romanticism and modern realism. The

first part reads like an early version of *A Portrait of the Artist As a Young Man*. Julien Sorel is portrayed as a bookish, sensitive young peasant, who is not quite sure whether he would prefer to be Pope or Emperor. He goes into the home of M. de Rênal, mayor of Verrières, as a tutor, and immediately seduces the mayor's beautiful wife. Later, when he moves to a still more aristocratic family, he seduces the proud and elegant daughter. In these activities, he retains the reader's sympathy; and the modern reader (who has probably encountered similar situations in *Sons and Lovers*, *Lucky Jim*, and *Room at the Top*), assumes that Julien has the author's sympathy, too. But here he will be mistaken. When, in a jealous fit, Julien attempts to shoot Mme. de Rênal and is executed, the author writes of his execution with no less detachment than that with which he wrote of the seductions. It is difficult to discern any unified artistic intention. Apparently Stendhal borrowed his plot from a contemporary newspaper scandal, so it is probable that Julien was condemned to death from the beginning. But in that case, one can only assume that the author allowed himself to be completely carried away in the earlier chapters, identifying himself with the struggles of his hero, and then got tired of writing and ended abruptly and without any apology. There is something lopsided and unbalanced about the book. The first part shows a real preoccupation with the struggle of a potential hero to find self-expression. Sartre has said that "to read a book is to rewrite it," and the reader of Stendhal feels himself challenged to imagine a future for Julien that is worthy of his ambition; he hopes that Stendhal will accept the challenge and show Julien's education and triumph in the minutest detail.

The abrupt ending comes as a shock; it leaves a feeling that the book is unfinished. *Le Rouge et le Noir* seems to be one half of a great novel. But after all, it is in the nineteenth-century tradition of tragedy and defeat. Perhaps we should be grateful to Stendhal for creating a real hero for the first two hundred pages, instead of being irritated that Julien becomes a papier-mâché figure for the last hundred.

The nineteenth century had re-created the hero. But above its Valhalla, in letters of gold, was inscribed the motto: "You can't win."

By the mid-nineteenth century, literature was already showing signs of a tendency towards other-direction. Dickens, Balzac, Flaubert, Turgenev, George Eliot were all more concerned with the individual as a social unit than with the romantic struggle for self-expression. Gogol really launched the cult of the ordinary chap when he made the hero of *The Overcoat* a harassed little clerk. His influence on later Russian writers was immense. Dostoevsky commented, "We have all emerged from under Gogol's overcoat."

One of the few exceptions was Herman Melville, who created in the character of Captain Ahab a hero who possessed strange affinities with Don Quixote. Ahab is unique; not so much because he is an exception to the rule that you can't win as because he knows he cannot, and doesn't care. In a sense, he is more important as a symbol than as an individual. (His chase after the white whale occasionally becomes tiresome.) What is important is his *absurd* courage. He illustrates an important point: that the hero's aims need not be reasonable — that, on the contrary, everything depends upon the act of will, the indomitable obsession, rather than upon the reasoned calculation. But although a logical positivist might see no clear distinction between Ahab and Don Quixote, the distinction is of fundamental importance. Don Quixote has no relation to any form of reality; he blunders on in a fog of romance. Ahab has also turned his back upon reality — insofar as his family and Starbuck and Stubb represent reality — but his will power reaches out where his imagination collapses. Although he also denies the "common daylight," although he knows that Moby Dick cannot be beaten, some giant act of obsession in him forces him onwards. As the wreckage of the *Pequod* subsides into the sea, there is no feeling of defeat; only of protest against the nineteenth-century assumption that you can't win, the premise that prevents writers from creating heroes who dare to assert any identity or sense of purpose beyond the society in which they live.

In France, the heroic was revived, to some extent, in the work of Guy de Maupassant, but mostly in the form of a debased Don Juanism. Five out of six of Maupassant's novels are about seduction; to enjoy them, the reader must identify himself with the hero and immerse himself in an atmosphere of high-minded eroticism (high-minded, for sex in Maupassant is never crude and physical; Joyce would undoubtedly have shocked him deeply). *Bel Ami*, one of the best of his novels, is in the tradition of *Le Rouge et le Noir*. It deals with the seductions and rogueries of an amiable but ambitious Casanova. It is not (as Tolstoy seemed to believe) a criticism of society, nor is Bel Ami intended as a villainous gigolo. Maupassant illustrates perfectly Blake's comment that all true poets are of the devil's party; he obviously derives great enjoyment

from describing how Bel Ami seduces the wife of his
employer, and then the daughter, and ends by marrying
the daughter (whose father is a millionaire) in a cathedral.
The reader also takes pleasure in Bel Ami's course from
penniless clerk to Chevalier of the Légion d'Honneur.
It is true that Bel Ami is not particularly intelligent or
sensitive; but then, none of Maupassant's heroes is.

But Bel Ami is the nearest Maupassant ever came to
that close self-identification with the hero that was so
typical of the romantic era. Even Tolstoy, on his moral
high horse, noticed it: "*Bel Ami* is a very dirty book. The
author evidently gives himself a free hand in describing
what attracts him, and at times seems to lose his main
negative attitude towards the hero and to pass over to his
side." In his later novels, Maupassant gives himself over
completely to writing of the pleasures of seduction, and
allows the hero no other motive in life. Increasingly, he
prefers to write about weaklings. All his novels are su-
perbly written, and all revolve around sex. (It is surprising,
in the circumstances, that there has been no enthusiastic
Maupassant revival in recent years.) But the novels lack
a center of gravity. Although the author declines to load
the dice against his heroes in the fashionable manner, he
also declines to try to represent them as in any way
admirable.

The amazing thing about the novels of the nineteenth
century — and it is even more true of the twentieth — is
that the writers seemed to feel no instinctive aversion to
loading the dice against their heroes. After all, imaginative
invention usually starts when a child tells himself tall
stories in which he figures as the hero. The essence of
fiction lies in this machinery of wish fulfillment, of vica-

rious pleasure, of the reader's identification of himself with the hero. How, in that case, can its aims be so completely altered? The answer lies partly in a writer's sense of drama, the need for theatrically effective situations. Maupassant's first short story, *Boule de Suif*, like his first novel, *Une Vie*, possesses a compassion and sense of pity that somehow do not ring true; they give the feeling that Maupassant has assumed them for the occasion, being on his best behavior as a young writer making his first bow to his audience. As soon as he felt more certain of himself, he also began to be true to himself and dropped the fashionable note of pity.

This is a fascinating problem of psychology. Consider Zola, for instance, the great preacher of realism. The reader might imagine that he was not a storyteller but a scientist classifying butterflies. There seems to be no trace of wish fulfillment in his sordid tragedies. The early novel, *Thérèse Raquin*, provides a perfect illustration of this paradox. It begins by involving the reader's interest in the fate of the orphan Thérèse, who lives with her aunt and invalid cousin in Paris. The household centers around the wretched invalid Camille Raquin, whose mother adores him. Thérèse becomes his wife and settles down to a stifled existence with the sallow-skinned, weakly mother's boy, who is a clerk in a store. Sometime later, Camille meets an old school friend, a muscular artist named Laurent, and introduces him into his home. Laurent decides to seduce Thérèse, and succeeds without much difficulty. The adultery is an immense release for Thérèse; it transforms her from the silent, bored companion into a woman with incredibly violent desires. The relation between Thérèse and Laurent becomes stronger, until they are insanely in love. They decide to murder Camille, so that they can marry. On a boating excursion, Laurent throws the husband overboard. The murder scene is followed by a chapter that can only be compared with Dostoevsky for power and horror, in which Laurent goes daily to the morgue to look for the corpse of Camille.

Up to this point, the novel moves with tremendous force, and the reader feels that Zola is fulfilling all the functions of a great artist. He has projected himself into the situation of a frustrated woman and has shown that frustration being swept away (one of the most dramatic and touching subjects in all art). But now Zola suddenly withdraws, and writes a conventional tragedy of conscience. Thérèse and Laurent marry, but the dead husband is always between them. Madame Raquin becomes paralyzed, and when she finally learns that her son was murdered, can only roll her eyes. Thérèse and Laurent simultaneously decide to murder one another; when they discover each other's design, both commit suicide. It is unconvincing and boring (for the harrowings of conscience go on for over half the book). Zola so plainly intends to harrow the reader that he has the opposite effect; he only alienates. The old woman's paralysis, which is obviously intended to be a knockout blow, produces the same effect as the accumulated brutalities of modern gangster fiction — it seems contrived, too deliberate. (This is also painfully true of what many consider to be Zola's best novel, *La Terre*.)

But why was there this sudden change of attitude halfway through the book? One is inclined to suspect that Zola's imagination failed him. He was challenged to show the effect of freedom on two people who had lived in an invisible prison. The feat was too much for him. He fell back on dramatic formulas, and the life went out of the novel.

But the reader who suspects Zola of lacking imagination has a hard case to prove. It is true that all his novels leave the feeling, "here is a man whose creative faculty is two-dimensional, flat, lacking the dimension of freedom," but Zola's air of being a scientist rather than a writer is intimidating. Critics lay great emphasis on the amount of research that went into the novels (just as early defenders of Joyce tried to give the impression that *Ulysses* is a highly erudite and esoteric work, on no account to be judged by ordinary standards). Zola seems to deny that all art is based on identification, wish fulfillment: he writes as a lepidopterist.

But when one examines Zola's life, this plea collapses. Most of the novels are dominated by sex — particularly by rape. Yet Zola led a highly respectable life. He took a mistress in his early years, married her, and remained faithful to her. The novels were full of sexual violence. Nevertheless, Zola led an exemplary life.

But when he was fifty, he fell in love with a girl of twenty-two and seduced her. Jeanne Rozerot was his wife's maid. The result was a love affair that lasted till the end of his life. And sex dropped abruptly out of the novels. The year before he met Jeanne, Zola had published *La Terre*, which has an atmosphere of sex and violence that resembles nothing so much as *No Orchids for Miss Blandish*. Immediately after the beginning of his affair with her, he wrote the beautiful and idyllic *Le Rêve*, and the delicate love story *Doctor Pascal*. It seems hardly necessary to argue that sex in the earlier books was a form of wish fulfillment.

I dwell on Zola because the realism for which his name

became a synonym has also become the basic premise of twentieth-century writing. This premise states that writing should be scientific — an observation and documentation of social facts. I would argue that writing never has been and never can be anything of the sort. At its center, there must be a completely personal statement of its author's attitude to life and to freedom. This attitude will manifest itself in the author's attitude towards the hero. If the author has no subjective strength, no sense of freedom, then his work will be broken-backed, no matter how imposing his realism makes it appear. In Zola's novels, as in *The Caine Mutiny,* society is the hero. Zola lacked the inner-direction, the inner reality, to create authentic heroes. The imposing façade is a fake.

All that emerges from consideration of the nineteenth century is that, with occasional exceptions, its writers lost sight of the hero. Society is the true hero of most nineteenth-century novels. The significance of Melville's Ahab, Dostoevsky's Underground Man, Goethe's Faust was completely lost on the disciples of Zola and George Eliot.

One of the most important exceptions, and one not generally considered as a character of fiction, is Nietzsche's Zarathustra. Nietzsche, who was in every way an inner-directed man, tried in Zarathustra to create the new hero. Zarathustra begins by turning his back on society and coming to grips with his own problems. We are told that he had passed through a period of utter pessimism and life-denial; he obviously feels the same as the Underground Man about the old hero, as his comments on the army and the state show clearly. What is most interesting about Zarathustra is Nietzsche's realization that the real hero must be a *perfectly healthy* man. Like Goethe, he does

not believe in weighting his hero with neuroses. But unlike Goethe, Nietzsche was not himself a physically healthy
person. The result is that Zarathustra shows the conflict
between Nietzsche's weakness and his own strength. In
some sections, Zarathustra speaks with the ecstasy and
certainty of a prophet; in others, he seems torn by self-
division. This work provides an insight into the difficulties
of a writer who wishes to create a completely heroic figure.
Nietzsche tried to portray the authentic hero — the man
who has passed through self-division to self-knowledge
and the power to act. Zarathustra is also a sort of wish-
fulfillment fantasy; he has perfect health, many disciples,
an unclouded vision. But his action amounts only to
preaching, and the world in which he preaches is an
anonymous realm of fantasy. Like Goethe's *Faust*, *Thus
Spake Zarathustra* is an attempt to create the new hero,
and an admission of failure.

I have already discussed, in *The Outsider*, the way in
which the idea of the "man on his own" began to be debased in the twentieth century. The defeat premise, the
hypothesis of insignificance, begins to obtrude itself all
the time. The solitary hero of Barbusse's *L'Enfer* is
gloomily modest: "I have nothing and I deserve nothing."
It is interesting to note the transition from *Faust,* through
the Underground Man. Faust had expressed pessimism
and despair as he sits alone in his room, but the despair has
nothing to do with society; it is to do with the problem of
the meaning of the "will to truth." He feels a certain
patronizing affection for society; he would like to take
refuge in the gaiety of the country folk on Easter day, but
knows he can never feel restored to kinship with other
men. The Underground Man is already morosely anti-

social, although the problems that oppress him are also problems about the will to truth, the strength and weakness of human beings. Like Zarathustra, he is inclined to regard men as "flies in the market place." But Barbusse's hero is simply anti-social — that and no more. Although he says: "Truth — what do they mean by it?" this is a cynical gesture of disillusionment rather than a real question. His problem is mainly his feeling of insignificance. "I have nothing and I deserve nothing. Yet I feel I deserve some recompense." But nothing can convince him that he is not insignificant.

The Last Stand of the Romantic Hero

In England, at the beginning of the twentieth century, there were a few last flickers of the heroic ideal. There was Kipling's "empire loyalism"; but this soured into a curious defeatism in his later work.* And there was an active interest in the intelligent hero in Wells, Chesterton, and Shaw. This appears most strongly in Chesterton, but he is also, unfortunately, the least serious. His temperament contained a mixture of mysticism, juvenile humor, and naïveté, in about equal parts. His idea of reviving the heroic was to plunge back into the past; *The Napoleon of Notting Hill* is a fantasy about a man who takes the ancient rivalries of the boroughs of London with deadly earnestness and starts a civil war to settle the question of precedence. Even Chesterton's politics was medieval; he advocated a feudal system of ownership (Distributism). Books such as *The Man Who Was Thursday, Manalive,*

* See "The Kipling Nobody Read" in Edmund Wilson's *The Wound and the Bow.*

The Ball and the Cross exploit his flamboyant vein of heroic romanticism.

Wells' contributions, although far more incidental to his major ideas, are a great deal more solid than Chesterton's. In a very early book, *Love and Mr. Lewisham,* he showed the young schoolmaster, Lewisham, thinking out a formidable campaign against the world, which begins at five every morning with three hours of French. He reckons that by the age of twenty-four he will have several modern languages and a broad all-round education, and be prepared for greater achievements. Unfortunately, Mr. Lewisham is no Julien Sorel; he falls in love and forgets the whole scheme. And yet Wells never seemed to be interested in the problem of the ambitious man, of the man doing battle with his circumstances. *The History of Mr. Polly* builds up a picture of a middle-aged man who has allowed himself to become completely oppressed by circumstances, and then shows him breaking the chain with one act of desperation (Mr. Polly's decision to commit suicide and burn down the house). The book is not a major work, and it is doubtful if Wells himself took it very seriously; yet it is an interesting contradiction of the nineteenth-century spirit of defeat, the Chekhovian pessimism. Wells had an immense store of vitality, and the optimism that went with it; unfortunately, like Chesterton, he failed to take himself seriously enough. In this they form an interesting contrast with the generation of Joyce, Eliot, and Hemingway that came after.

Shaw is an altogether more serious writer than Chesterton or Wells, although, like them, he wrote too much and often wrote hastily and carelessly. Even so, his Julius Caesar in *Caesar and Cleopatra* is the only serious attempt in twentieth-century literature to create an undefeated hero. And Shaw faced squarely the metaphysical issues that defeated Faust and the Underground Man. In the Don Juan in Hell scene of *Man and Superman,* Juan can say, "As long as I can conceive something better than myself, I cannot be easy unless I am striving to bring it into existence," and speaks of "the work of helping life in its struggle upwards."

This is far more significant than might appear on a first reading. The ancient Greek hero was a mortal who hoped to gain the favor of the gods, and the medieval knight was a mortal who trusted to his patron saint and Jesus. Faust is the man who objects to being mortal. His whole quest is aimed at becoming godlike; his despair lies in his inability to escape his own miserable limitations. Now Shaw continues in the Faustian tradition, making Don Juan state: "Life is a force which has made innumerable experiments in organizing itself." "The mammoth and the man, the mouse and the megatherium . . . are all more or less successful attempts to build up that raw force into higher and higher individuals, the ideal individual being omnipotent, omniscient, infallible, and withal completely unilludedly self-conscious; in short, a god." The issue is now plain. The old hero was the favorite of the gods; the new hero aims at becoming a god. Riesman would say that the old hero was tradition-directed, while the new hero aims at being completely inner-directed.

Shaw was the only thinker of his generation to face the ultimate religious issues. He saw clearly that the problem of the hero lies in the fact that nothing a man can do outlasts his own life, that death makes all achievement seem futile. An age of belief could set its hopes on heaven, while

liberal humanism contented itself with phrases that concealed the defeat: "A man lives in his descendants," "An
artist's life begins after his death," and so forth. But with
the reality of death and corruption hanging over life, the
question "What shall we do with our lives?" has no more
importance than "Do you prefer light ale or brown?" and
all philosophy becomes a waste of time. Plato and the
Buddha answered the question by saying that man returns to earth repeatedly, so that death is an illusion (and
their answer appears to have satisfied many modern intellectuals, Aldous Huxley and Christopher Isherwood
among them). Shaw decided that men have more con-
trol over their lives than they realize (the answer is typical
of him) and that they could live indefinitely if they made
the effort. Whether his answer is regarded as satisfactory
or not, he had recognized the problem and made his attempt to solve it; in doing so, he had taken up the problem
of the hero where Goethe had left it.

The chief objection to Shaw's method of dramatic dia-
logue is that it cannot command the conviction of Zola-
like realism. The only purpose of realism, after all, is to
be convincing. In some ways, the technique of realism
might be compared to that of music; this can be seen
clearly by considering a book such as Joyce's *Ulysses,* which
apparently adheres strenuously to the conventions of realism, never aiming for dramatic effects, never trying to
move the reader by arguments, but whose final effect is
like that of music or great poetry — overpowering emotional conviction of the value of life. But at the same time,
Joyce can never "say" as much as the third act of *Man and
Superman.* Each method has its advantages, and the greatest writer is the man who can combine the best of both.

But this is precisely what did *not* happen when a new literary generation followed the generation of Wells and Chesterton. Idealism was out; realism was in, and Joyce, Huxley, Anderson, Sinclair, Hemingway, Dos Passos deliberately excluded any general ideas from their work and plunged deep into the "fallacy of insignificance" and the cult of the ordinary chap. Aldous Huxley, in particular, specialized in the cringing hero, the "chinless intelligent man," as if to compensate for his audacity in interweaving a few ideas. Down to his most recent novel (*The Genius and the Goddess*) he seems incapable of writing about a hero without an inferiority complex.

It is true that, unlike most novelists of the twentieth century, Huxley possesses a real sense of values and uses the novel to propagate it. But the values are intellectual, and they affect his writing only on the intellectual level. Physically and emotionally, the insignificance premise dominates. Even the reader who sympathizes with Huxley's ideas will feel a sense of incompleteness about his world. It ignores so many aspects of living experience that any navvy or Woolworth's shopgirl would know intimately. Only an other-directed intellectual could find Huxley's picture of the world adequate, for the Huxley hero is always intellectual and always painfully aware of other people. Without unfairness, Huxley might be called the prophet of the other-directed intellectual.

Literary Faking

The question of literary values provides an interesting side light on the problems of other-direction. The mass manipulation by advertisers has its respectable cultural counterpart in writers such as Graham Greene, Evelyn Waugh, D. H. Lawrence. These writers have a set of values, and their purpose is to impose these values on their readers. To do this, they use a method that deserves to be considered as an additional chapter to *The Hidden Persuaders*. It consists in making the fullest use of literary realism. Greene and Waugh are both orthodox Roman Catholics, and the change in technique becomes immediately apparent if one contrasts them with an earlier Catholic apologist, Paul Claudel. In what many consider to be his finest play, *Le Soulier de Satin,* Claudel makes the most sweeping demands on his audience; there is very little conventional dramatic action, and the play moves forward in a series of long speeches that require close attention. Greene and Waugh, on the contrary, take care to give the public what it wants and attempt to slip in their propaganda at a level where it will hardly be noticed. The result produces in many unprejudiced readers the effect of a literary confidence trick.

Greene's method, for instance, follows a well-established pattern. He begins by portraying his characters and the world they live in with an apparently ruthless frankness. There is a heavy emphasis on sex, sordidness, and humiliation. The reader has a feeling that Greene is turning to him periodically and asking: "Am I trying to fake anything? Have I told any lies?" And the reader, crushed and impressed, answers: "No, go on." The picture builds up with appalling inevitability, selecting details of human sin, weakness, and misery — and entirely omitting any reference to the strength or poetry of human existence. If the reader has been carried along and convinced, the final effect is to make him feel that the world is a far worse place than he had ever imagined. And once this idea is firmly established, he is in the right frame of mind to appreciate Greene's patent remedy: Catholicism. "Don't worry, the world may be an awful dump, but the mercy of God is infinite," and so forth. For the reader who feels inclined to ask, "But what about Beethoven, what about Michelangelo and Van Gogh and Rabelais . . . ?" there is no reply, and he is left with a guilty suspicion that perhaps he is rather immature to ask such questions.

The work of D. H. Lawrence, although at its best it touches greatness, often degenerates into the same kind of thing — in *St. Mawr* and *Lady Chatterley's Lover,* for instance. People are portrayed as stupid, or mean and envious, or hopelessly trivial, and once the reader has been convinced that the world Lawrence presents is a faithful picture of the world in which we all live, he is prepared to agree with Lawrence that things are in a pretty bad way. All that remains is the sale of the patent remedy — in this case, sex.

The type of literary confidence trick that some Soviet Russian authors specialize in adopts roughly the same method — the emphasis upon the delights of communal living, the need for every man to be a good member of the community, the horrors and injustices of capitalism, and so forth. As in the work of Greene and Lawrence, it depends on the reader's not possessing enough imagination to envisage a higher destiny for the hero (and, by implication, for himself) than the one the author has selected for him — collective farming, the Catholic church, or being Lady Chatterley's lover.

All these writers present a selected range of human

experience as if it were completely representative. Like any other confidence trick, their work depends for the success of its message upon the gullibility of the audience, and in this case, the gullibility is the immediate result of other-direction.

A European Hero in the Twentieth Century

When asked his opinion of modern American writing, André Gide is reported to have said: "American literature is soulless." His meaning is clear, although the wording is ambiguous (after all, continental literature could hardly be called "soulful"). What Gide meant, undoubtedly, is that American literature is not subjective enough. But even if the European novel has not yet become "society conscious" to the same extent as the American novel, the unheroic premise still hovers in the background, the unsolved metaphysical heritage of Goethe and Dostoevsky.

One of the most interesting heroes in twentieth-century literature is Ulrich, the hero of Robert Musil's *Der Mann ohne Eugenschaften* (*The Man without Qualities*). Musil was an engineer-turned-writer, whose training had been largely military. The extremely interesting result is already visible in his early autobiographical novel, *Die Verwirrungen des Zoglings Törless* (*The Perplexities of Young Törless*). The novel deals with Musil's period at Weisskirchen, the military school at which Rilke had been so miserable. But although *Törless* has something in common with other novels about young artists, it is a far tougher book than the average. If compared with Rilke's fragments about the same school (*The Gymnastic Lesson* and *Pierre Dumont*) Musil's toughness appears almost as ruthlessness.

Musil's only other novel is the immense *The Man without Qualities*. In some ways, this is one of the most disconcerting books ever written, an extraordinary mixture of great writing and long-winded word-spinning. Musil has a preference for indirect narrative and a ponderous prose style that reads like a mixture of Dickens and Kant. The plot is concerned mainly with a great patriotic campaign run by a number of silly, cultured people, and Ulrich's involvement in it. The satire is heavy going. Anatole France is quoted as saying "Art is long but Proust is longer," but the bon mot is even more applicable to Musil. His indirect style makes a two-thousand-page book seem like four thousand.

But having said all this, it must be admitted that it is the only twentieth-century novel that at times speaks with the power and authority of Dostoevsky. The greatest sections are all concerned with Ulrich, the "man without qualities," and his complex personal life. Ulrich is an older version of Törless. He is a man who has never for a moment doubted that it is his destiny to do something great. But he has no idea of what he will do. "He saw wonderfully clearly that . . . he had in himself all the abilities and qualities favored by the time in which he lives; but he had somehow lost the capacity to apply them." Like Faust, Ulrich is young and personally attractive, as well as being fairly rich. He has been in the army and has lived a fast life of seduction, drinking, and fighting duels. When the army disappointed his incorrigible romanticism (he had challenged a financier to a duel, and the financier had Ulrich reprimanded by his colonel, thus revealing that money counted for more than courage, even in the Austrian army), he resigned his commission and became an engineer. Even this was pure romanticism; he imagined the engineer as the superman of the modern world (an illusion that still persists in Soviet Russia, to judge by its novels). When he discovered that engineers are no more intelligent or stupid than most people, he became a mathematician, his romanticism having now led him to believe that mathematical truth is pure truth and that the mathematician is the modern equivalent of the wizard. He soon became disillusioned again. This terminates his three attempts to become a "man of importance." When the novel opens, this stage of his career is already behind him. A mature man stands on the threshold of life, a man armed with the intellect of a mathematician, the subtlety of a philosopher, the sensitivity of a poet, and the physical attractions of a Don Juan. With these qualities, one might expect an extraordinary career for Ulrich; his creator had in his hands the possibility of a rich and exciting narrative. The actuality is disappointing. Ulrich merely gets involved in a preposterous nationalistic campaign and has several love affairs. In spite of his heroic qualities, there is nothing to be done.

What, then, is Musil's achievement as a novelist?

In some ways, it can be compared to Proust's. Proust brought a new slow-motion sensitivity to the novel, one that is able to analyze emotions with infinite subtlety. Musil brings a slow-motion intellect to it, one that reveals the strange ambiguities of consciousness, the extraordinary complexity of modern life. He satirizes the generals and financiers and "cultured" hostesses involved in the great patriotic campaign; they have "explained" life on a number of absurdly simple assumptions that fail to give even the least idea of its complexity. These people all act and speak with certainty because they are stupid. Ulrich, who never loses a sense of the ambiguity of reality, is a man without qualities because his tolerance is too broad to pass judgment. He prefers to remain a young man of promise because he sees too deeply to commit himself irrevocably to any course of action; he would rather be a man with a thousand potential achievements than a man with one actual achievement that has canceled out all the others.

Musil's theme is the twentieth century, its speed and complexity; some of his early chapters read like an anticipation of *The Organization Man*. His novel is also an exposure of the outworn fallacies, the absurd oversimplifications, on which our streamlined society runs. A great deal of the book is devoted to Moosbrugger, the sexual maniac who has been sentenced to death although he is plainly unbalanced. Ulrich feels a strange kinship with Moosbrugger. This is not because Ulrich feels himself to be a potential sex maniac (although he recognizes a savagely irrational element in himself that could express itself in murder), but because both he and Moosbrugger are men with a deep and complex vision of the human soul and both feel helpless rage at the stupid oversimplifications upon which society bases its judgments. For Ulrich, the fact that society is stupid makes no great difference; but Moosbrugger its stupidity condemns to death. Moosbrugger's situation bears some resemblance to Meursault's in Camus's *L'Etranger;* Ulrich cannot help feeling, "There but for the grace of God go I."

Musil never finished the novel (which is perhaps just

as well, since it is doubtful whether any reader would
have succeeded in doing so). This is unimportant. He
had re-created the Faust figure in a typically modern context (1913-1914), and this was a very considerable achievement for the period between the wars, when the unheroic
premise dominated the literature of Europe and America.

In this book, I am deliberately paying very little attention to Proust, for obvious reasons. If his hypochondriac
Marcel is to be seriously considered as a hero, then the
word "hero" is almost meaningless. Marcel suffers from
an acute form of the insignificance fallacy. In *Swann's
Way,* he relates how his mother stayed the night in his
room and "permanently weakened his will." All through
the book, he is never wholly free of a feeling of self-contempt. Defenders of Proust might argue that this reveals
self-knowledge. I am more inclined to believe that it
shows self-deception, the weakness of a man who is too
lazy to make any effort to discipline himself. He suffers
from the notion that sensitivity must involve various kinds
of weakness. Since Goethe and Musil have both created
striking disproofs of this, Proust's argument will convince
only other hypochondriacs. This is not to dismiss Proust,
but only to say that his work is irrelevant in this context.

The same can be said of nearly all the work of Thomas
Mann. The central thesis of Mann's novels is that the artist
is somehow unfitted for life. This conviction gathered
strength as he grew older. Finally, his feeling of the need
for solidarity and balance led him to exalt the bourgeois
as the salvation of the modern world, although the "unbalanced" artist continued to have a morbid fascination
for him. But his tetralogy, *Joseph and His Brothers,* provides an important exception. In this book, Mann writes

about the old hero, the "lucky" man. In Greek mythology, to be lucky meant to be favored by the gods. The same concept lies behind the stories of knights in the Middle Ages, and it is invisibly present in the *Arabian Nights*. Joseph, like Ulrich, is born with all the qualities for greatness; unlike Ulrich, he is not a modern hero, which means that there is no obstacle to prevent him from fulfilling his destiny. On this level, the story is simple and straightforward. Its main interest lies in the fact that Joseph is an authentic hero figure, an exception to the unheroic premise.

[handwritten margin note: NOT A MODERN HERO HAS NO OBSTACLE TO PREVENT HIM FROM FULFILLING HIS DESTINY (THE WAY THE NOVELIST THINKS— WHILE MODERN HERO GOES THRU OBSTACLES) ?]

Part Four

The Fallacy
of Insignificance

THE STATEMENT that Ulrich and Moosbrugger feel a helpless rage at the oversimplifications upon which society bases its judgments summarizes the central preoccupation of existentialism. Existentialism is an attempt to map and explore human complexity; its chief *bête noire* is oversimplification (or abstraction).

The word was first used to describe a philosophical attitude by Sören Kierkegaard, who defined it in his assertion: "Truth is subjectivity." The oversimplification that Kierkegaard rebelled against was German metaphysics, with its claims to "explain" history and the world. Since Kierkegaard, the label has been applied to a great many thinkers — Heidegger, Jaspers, Marcel, Sartre, and Camus are the best-known names. Of these, only the last two now accept the term "existentialist" as a description of their attitude. At one stage, Marcel called himself a "Christian existentialist," but most existentialists would agree that the terms are self-contradictory (at least, if Christianity is defined as belief in redemption from Original Sin by Christ). Heidegger and Jaspers have shown themselves true to the spirit of existentialism by preferring to write about poets and artists rather than to discuss philosophy; Heidegger has written penetratingly on Höl-

derlin and Nietzsche, and Jaspers has also written about
Nietzsche, as well as about Van Gogh and Rilke.

Existentialism has an immediate bearing upon the problem of the hero. Its concepts provide the tools with which
the whole problem can be dissected. The present section
will be devoted to an attempt to define these concepts,
particularly as they appear in the work of Sartre and
Camus.

A Philosophy of Inner-Direction

Sartre's existentialism could be called a philosophy of
inner-direction. Its aim is to emphasize man's freedom
and to explain the workings of that freedom.

In Hemingway's short story, "The Short Happy Life of
Francis Macomber," Macomber is a coward who has run
away from a charging lion, leaving the white hunter to
deal with it. His wife is so contemptuous of him that she
is unfaithful with the white hunter and makes no attempt
to conceal it. Later, as they are shooting buffalo, Macomber is carried away by his excitement and stands up to a
charging buffalo. His wife also shoots at the buffalo and
accidentally hits Macomber, killing him. Macomber's
"short happy life" was the time between regaining his
courage and receiving a bullet in the brain. Sartre would
say that during his "short happy life" Macomber existed
authentically, and that during the period when he considered himself a coward he existed *inauthentically.* Man
is free. This means he cannot be a coward in the same
way, for instance, that a table is a table. He may be a
coward on some particular occasion, but every new occasion
that presents itself offers him a completely clean sheet, to

be a coward again, or to be a hero. Observe that I used the phrase "be a coward *again*" rather than "continue to be a coward." He may have acted like a coward on *every* occasion, yet it is still not true to say he *is* a coward. He is free. He can even decide "I am not a coward" when he has not yet *proved* he is not a coward, for in his essence he has no qualities. In his essence he is not even a man; he just *is*.

Now, obviously, the statement "a man is free" is almost meaningless if it is taken to mean "he has no limitations." In order to have meaning, his limitations must be stated, the boundaries within which he has freedom and choice.

To begin with, Sartre means that there are no laws of God which must be obeyed, for there is no God. His existentialism is atheistic. (Atheism, however, is not a necessary premise of existentialism.) This also applies to all so-called sacred books and revelations. The kind of premise laid down by the Jehovah's Witnesses, for instance — "The Bible is the only reliable source of truth" — would be dismissed instantly by any existentialist as the most fundamental kind of error. When a man begins to look outside himself for his freedom, he has already plunged into inauthentic living, and his thinking is unsound in its foundations. But there is another important way in which men surrender their freedom: in slavery to their own pasts. If a man assumes he is a coward, because he has committed a dozen acts of cowardice, or if he feels that he is a sinner who must repent, then he is imposing the strait jacket of his past upon his present freedom. In Sartre's play, *Les Mouches* (*The Flies*), Orestes murders Clytemnestra and refuses to repent, even when it means being hunted for the rest of his life by the Furies. While he acknowledges the act, he has his freedom. Once he disowns the act, or tries to explain it away (as Zeus persuades Electra to disown her part in the crime by telling her she never really *meant* to murder), he has destroyed his own freedom, chained himself voluntarily. Zeus puts on a show which is reminiscent of the book of Job, pointing to the stars, the sea, the earth, trying to overawe Orestes, demanding: "Who created you?" Orestes replies: "You did. But you made one mistake. You created me free."*

There is a third way in which a man can lose his freedom — through self-deception (*mauvaise-foi*). This is by far the most important way, and a huge proportion of Sartre's work explores the varieties of self-deception. *Portrait of an Anti-Semite,* for instance, deals with the form of self-deception involved in anti-Semitism. One of his finest short stories, "Childhood of a Leader," is a brilliant parable of *mauvaise-foi*. It deals with the childhood and youth of a boy, Lucien Fleurier, who possesses the sensitivity of the young Proust or Joyce (Sartre was greatly influenced by Joyce, as well as by Faulkner) and an intellectual subtlety that makes him wonder, at one point, whether there is any proof that he exists. He has a difficult adolescence, suffering from shyness, inability to express himself, and various complexes and worries. He reads Rimbaud and Freud and is deeply impressed by both.

---

* There is hardly any need here to point out the similarity of Sartre's doctrine to the quietism of Molinos (which the church condemned as a heresy): the belief that repentance is a waste of time, that a man had better decide to do better next time and forget about his "sins." Sri Ramakrishna preached the same: "It is the mind that makes one bound or emancipated." Shaw's dictum that a man should have the courage of his vices is still another approach to the same belief. It is pointless to accuse Sartre of unoriginality. In philosophy, all thought is common property; what matters is the light that each individual is able to shed on it.

Later he comes under the domination of a homosexual
professor, who seduces him. This is the climax of his
feeling of total lostness. He doesn't know who he is, or
what he wants out of life. He knows he is sensitive and
intelligent, but these qualities lead nowhere. He has no
conviction of any sort. He does not even know whether he
is a homosexual, although the fact that he has had a homosexual experience inclines him to believe that he is. (Note
here Sartre's doctrine of inauthentic existence.) But he
begins to mix with a violent set of right-wing young people,
anti-Semites and devotees of *L'Action Française,* the right-
wing newspaper. Their gaiety and lightly carried conviction enchant him. Soon he becomes the most passionate
of anti-Semites and right-wingers. Even so, his anti-
Semitism is in the nature of a tryout, like looking at oneself in a new hat in the mirrors of a hat shop. He has not
yet *identified* himself with it. But an incident changes his
attitude. He has two friends — a youth named Guigard
and his attractive sister Pierrette. Lucien suspects the
sister of being a little in love with him, and the suspicion
has a delightful effect on his vanity. They invite him to
a party, at which there happens to be a Jewish friend of the
Guigards. Guigard tries to introduce Lucien to the Jew;
Lucien turns his back and walks out of the house. Immediately, he feels ashamed of himself, and overwhelmed
with embarrassment and self-pity. He has thrown away
two friends for the sake of a stupid principle. He is on the
point of returning to apologize, but he feels even more
shame at the thought of an apology. Finally, after a night
of misery, he decides to apologize to the friend the next
day. But when he sees Guigard at school, it is his friend
who apologizes first, and congratulates Lucien on his

strength of character. It becomes apparent that the admiration of Guigard's sister has also been intensified by the
incident. In a daze of well-being, he goes into a café and
thinks about it. He is *a person* at last. He imagines a
broad back marching away from a Jew, while Pierrette
Guigard and her brother stare after it with astonishment
and admiration, and thinks "That back is *me*, Lucien,
the Jew-hater." At last, he has a direction and a conviction.
He can *act;* he has a purpose. He can become a leader of
the right-wing movement eventually. Perhaps the dictator
of France. He imagines the woman who will be his — a
hero-worshiping child who belongs to him alone. When
he walks out of the café, he can hardly walk straight for
exaltation. He *is*. All doubts are behind him.

The story is an overwhelmingly ironical comment on
the times. (It is more ironical when one realizes that the
war followed, and the ultimate defeat of French reaction.)
Lucien has become a "person" by selling his freedom in
the subtlest way: to a stupid purpose. It is obvious that
Sartre sees him as only one degree removed from the opium
addict, and two degrees from the habitual drunkard. The
reader who knows his Hemingway will here be reminded
of "The Gambler, the Nun and the Radio": "Religion is
the opium of the people, economics is the opium of the
people," and so on with sex, patriotism, politics, the radio,
and so forth. But Hemingway's cripple is a complete
nihilist; he rejects all values. In Sartre's story, Lucien's
politics is an opium, a self-deception, but this does not
mean that all politics, all beliefs, are self-deception. But
where does the boundary lie? Why is Lucien's fascism
self-deception when Sartre's socialism is, presumably,
not? Partly because Lucien uses it deliberately as an ego

booster (after all, he had shown double weakness after the party: weakness of repenting what he has just done, and weakness of being too ashamed to try and undo it). But apart from this, Sartre never explains with any precision how he makes the leap from his view of fascism as self-deception to the socialism he has embraced. (Neither did Anatole France, for that matter, although he died a communist, after spending a lifetime ridiculing fanaticism.) This is one of the major flaws in Sartre's attitude to his work.

Existential Psychology

But what is most interesting in Sartre is his psychology — or, as he prefers to call it, his psychoanalysis. This is certainly his major contribution to contemporary thought. He calls this "existential psychoanalysis," and occasionally speaks as if Freud is an impostor and a late-comer to the field.

The basis of Sartre's psychology is his statement, in the one-act play, *Huis Clos* (*No Exit*), "Hell is other people." The play is the story of three people who wake up in hell, which turns out to be a large drawing room. There are no torments. But the three people seem to have been carefully chosen to get on one another's nerves. They are condemned to spend eternity in each other's company, never sleeping, never even being allowed to close their eyes. It is torture by triviality and boredom. Hell is an eternity of triviality. (There are echoes of Shaw's hell here.) One of the three is a man who enjoys meditation, but he will never be allowed to meditate, for he is in the company of a beautiful woman who craves his attention and a lesbian who is jealous of him. No general conclusions are stated, but they are clearly implied: man's greatest moments are moments of intense subjectivity, self-certainty, concentration. His greatest enemy is pointlessness, lack of purpose. Other people are the main problem. ("Increasingly, other people are the problem," David Riesman wrote of the other-directed character.) A man who is robbed of his subjectivity has nothing left.

In *L'Être et le Néant* (*Being and Nothingness*), Sartre's longest philosophical work, this problem is analyzed at great length. Sartre begins with the rather puzzling statement, "Man knows his consciousness as a nothingness." (One of the chief faults of Sartre's philosophical writing is a tendency to state things more abstractly than is strictly necessary.) And yet its meaning is simple enough. A man is very seldom aware of himself as a person; what he *is* mainly aware of, when he thinks of himself, is what other people think of him. I know that I change my character like a chameleon according to the person to whom I am talking. If I am talking to a pretty and very feminine girl, I feel positive and masculine. If I am speaking to some oppressively masculine man, I tend to feel negative and feminine. If I am talking to some old and famous author, who is pulling his age on me, I feel young and rebellious. If I am speaking to some very young and inexperienced writer, I am inclined to feel as if I am ninety-nine, with a life's work behind me. Although I know that none of these is the real Colin Wilson, that all are mirages called into existence by the character of the person I am speaking to, I cannot dismiss them and feel differently. (Eugene O'Neill deals with this theme in *The Great God Brown,* in which the characters put on different masks to signify their changes in character.)

Although all men know they exist (or take it for granted), they very seldom feel a solid kernel in themselves which they know to be the "real" Smith or Jones. What they know as "themselves" is this changing mirage caused by other people. One could go further and say that man usually experiences himself as a vacuum in his social environment. Hence Sartre's use of the word "nothingness" (vacuity).

But there are certain moments in which man knows himself as a positive reality; Francis Macomber knew it as he faced a charging buffalo without fear. In such moments of insight, a man knows he *exists,* he has an experience of freedom. But the moment does not bring the freedom *into existence*. It brings to the man awareness of a permanently present factor, just as a man only occasionally becomes aware of his own breathing, although his breathing never stops.

The result of this recognition is a knowledge of the dual nature of freedom. Man is free all the time, but he confronts his freedom only at long intervals. Between these occasions, he is free, but does not know it. To be free without knowing it is not to be free. In order to become a reality which authenticates existence, freedom must be grasped intuitively.   قيمة كل ذات تتوقف على قيمة حريتها !

The chief obstacle to intuitive apprehension is self-division, for the self-divided man is aware of himself as an intellect, a personality, rather than as an urge to live. Even on the simplest level, modern man is bound to be self-divided, for in his life he must be involved in a large

BECAUSE OF
o MANY,   سبب انقسامه على ذاته هو المعرفة والخبرة !
UNNECESSARY DELUSIONS
بسبب المعلومات الكثيرة.

amount of repetitious routine. While he is automatically performing these routine operations, his thoughts and feelings will tend to pursue their own course. Hence, on the simplest level, he is self-divided. (The disciplines of Taoism and Zen regard this as an evil, and demand that the adept should concentrate his whole being on everything he does.) Under these conditions, freedom is anything that will unite the whole being in one apprehension. In his long novel, *Les Chemins de la Liberté* (*The Roads to Freedom*), Sartre makes his hero reflect: "Freedom is terror." But Yeats and Rupert Brooke had approached the same insight when they spoke of the liberating effect of the urge to flight, Brooke in the sonnet "Now God be thanked . . ." and Yeats in "Under Ben Bulben":

> Know that when all words are said
> And a man is fighting mad,
> Something drops from eyes long blind,
> He completes his partial mind,
> For an instant stands at ease,
> Laughs aloud, his heart at peace.

Freedom is not merely terror; it is *any* intense emotion that restores a man's subjectivity. The enemy is repetition, for it makes for self-division. The central character of *Les Chemins de la Liberté* is a university professor named Mathieu, a man whose deepest urge is towards freedom, or "salvation" as Sartre expresses it in the first volume (*L'Âge de Raison*). In pursuance of this aim, he has spent his life avoiding responsibilities. When his mistress is about to have a baby, he refuses to marry her, although they have been lovers for several years and she is, to all intents and purposes, his wife. This desire for freedom has not made an extraordinary man of him; on the contrary, he feels unreal, empty, purposeless. When he compares himself with his communist friend, Brunet, he feels only half-alive; Brunet has conviction, idealism, purpose. The situation repeats the elements of *Notes from Underground:* Mathieu subtle yet negative, Brunet stupid yet positive. Sartre makes no important advances on Dostoevsky's conclusions, and the over-all effect of the novel is as depressing as Dos Passos' *U.S.A.* (by which it seems to have been influenced in technique).

I am writing of Sartre at some length because he is the dramatist of "insignificance." In his novels, plays, and philosophical works, he analyzes every possible aspect of man's uncertainty. *La Nausée* is about a man who feels so insignificant that even objects overwhelm him. In *L'Être et le Néant* he speaks of those moments when a man is robbed of every shred of his subjectivity and exists completely as an object for other people. (The example Sartre gives is of a man being caught looking through a keyhole: in his feeling of guilt, he sees himself entirely *as the other person sees him,* and does not "exist for himself" in any way.) A man can be robbed of his reality in a thousand different ways — even a wet Monday morning causes a slump of the feelings that starts the self-division — and Sartre's analysis touches on most of them.

What Is to Be Done?

But his limitations appear when it comes to a question of a remedy. It might be objected that becoming fully conscious of the disease is at least half the battle, but this only makes the need for a solution more obvious. Sartre's solutions are the most dubious part of his analysis. It is true that he does not offer "solutions" in the way that Billy Graham or Karl Marx does. Nevertheless, he speaks of "commitment," of the "need to choose," and, finally, of the working-class movement as if they provided the answers for the problems he has expounded in such detail. After the war Sartre had a great deal of success as a lecturer and demonstrated his ability to stir his audience to intense enthusiasm; he expounded the doctrine that man is free and that each individual has to assert his freedom by "choosing." It is reported that his audiences left the hall fired with determination to alter their lives but that the enthusiasm never lasted long because Sartre had omitted to tell them *what* to choose, and they too had no idea. This pinpoints the weakness of Sartre's existentialism. It is a little too close to the vagueness of romantic revolt, as typified in *The Robbers*. "Choose anything, so long as you choose." In its method, his analysis bears close resemblances to that of Gurdjieff. There is the same emphasis on psychology and human self-deception. But Gurdjieff made an attempt to prescribe certain disciplines by which a man might establish his "inner reality." Sartre is less precise. He declares that a man must learn to become a member of the community, but never to relinquish his inner-direction. Like Whyte, he would probably advise the organization man to defy the organization as often as possible (although he fails to make clear what happens when the organization is a totalitarian government).

But the final index to an author's insight into inner-direction is his ability to write of the inner-directed man, the hero. For the most part, Sartre's central characters are as negative as those of any American novelist. There are two important exceptions: Orestes, in *Les Mouches,* whose defiance of Zeus in the last act has a purity of purpose that makes it one of Sartre's most moving works, and Goetz, the hero of *Le Diable et le Bon Dieu,* a man who proves his transcendence of concepts of good and evil by showing his ability to devote himself first to evil, then to good, then to evil again, with complete wholeheartedness, and thus to demonstrate the freedom of his will. But considered as his most important and ambitious work, *Les Chemins de la Liberté* has nothing to add to his analysis of freedom, and might almost have been written in America by an American. The promise of Dostoevskian power contained in *La Nausée* and *Les Mouches* is not justified in his longest novel.

It is not easy to decide just where along the line the failure occurred. But it is certain that it has to do with the connection between his politics and his existentialism. In an interview in *Les Nouvelles Littéraires* in 1951, he admitted that before the war his attitude had been relatively unpolitical; he supported the idea of democracy because it seemed to guarantee most freedom for the writer. But the war, his internment in Germany, his work in the resistance, produced a change of heart. He decided to become a "militantly democratic writer." He had already demonstrated an instinctive distaste for the bourgeois in *La Nausée* and *Le Mur;* when he launched *Les Temps Modernes* in 1945, he declared himself for the social revolution, the working classes, and the Communist Party. In *What is Literature?* he declares, "I know there is no other salvation for man than in the liberation of the working classes." Obviously, "salvation" here has quite a different meaning from the salvation that Mathieu dreams about.

What must be quite plain to any sympathetic reader of Sartre is that there is no real connection between his philosophy and his politics. His philosophy deals basically with the great hero problems and brings a new psychological subtlety to bear on the Faust dilemma. But Sartre is also a writer of considerable ambition, one who feels a desire to be a writer of his time in every sense. The impressive range of his work bears witness to this — novels, plays, short stories, philosophical treatises, argumentative pamphlets, literary criticism, political journalism — as well as his reply to a young admirer who asked him what makes a good writer: "Moral seriousness." His energies appear to be so broad and adaptable that it is hardly surprising that he should plunge into politics. *Les Temps Modernes* has taken a firm left-wing stand on political matters for the past fourteen years. Sartre has never been a member of the Communist Party and has on occasions been bitterly attacked by them for criticizing their old-fashioned materialism and political incompetence. The French Communists have labeled him, at various times, a Trotsky fascist hyena, a decadent bourgeois, a slimy rat, and a lubricious viper. But Sartre has always shown a great tolerance towards these attacks and has frequently formed an alliance with the Communists in particular campaigns (against the present De Gaulle government, for example, although in this case his intervention was late). When he was interviewed by the Paris *Express* at the time of the Hungarian rising, he was not afraid to say: "What the Hungarian people are teaching us with their blood is the complete failure of socialism as a Soviet-imported product."

This emphasis on politics has inevitably weakened Sartre as a philosopher and creative writer. As Philip Thody has pointed out, his attempts to defend the left have always lacked creative drive, while his attack on communist ideas, *Les Mains Sales,* is a tour de force. Worse still, Sartre's notions of commitment seem to have led to the idea that satire is the best medium for attacking the French right, and his latest play, *Nekrassov* (1955), is his weakest yet (it deals with a confidence trickster who poses as a Soviet government official who has escaped through the iron curtain).

The obvious complaint against Sartre is that he has ceased to be an existentialist. If "truth is subjectivity," then he has become steadily less concerned with truth since 1945. The Sartre of pre-war days, whose psychological explorations held promise that he might become a French Dostoevsky, has become a political commentator. His positive achievement remains in his early analyses of the varieties of human self-deception. Whether his political interests will produce works of literary importance still remains to be seen.

The Contribution of Camus

The position of Albert Camus provides some interesting contrasts with Sartre's. One of the most obvious differences between the two exponents of existentialism is a temperamental one: Camus is an Algerian with a deeply ingrained love of physical life. Therefore, the tension in his work has tended to stretch between two basic attitudes: a feeling of the absurdity and misery of human life, and intense physical affirmation of it. (A reader who comes to Sartre for the first time is struck by the sense of physical disgust;

I have said elsewhere that no other writer gives such an oppressive sensation of the mind being trapped in physical filth.)

This is an interesting starting point for a writer. There is an obvious connection between the idea of the heroic and physical affirmation. It is difficult to imagine a hero who finds the physical world disgusting. Sartre is like Aldous Huxley in his attitude of detachment from physical reality; Camus is far closer to Hemingway.*

Camus's earliest work shows his love of physical reality; it is there in his early essays, *L'Envers et L'Endroit* and *Noces*. In a preface written in 1958, he speaks of the unique source in every artist that "feeds all that he is and all he says," and declares, "Pour moi, je sais que ma source est dans *L'Envers et L'Endroit,* dans ce monde de pauvreté et de lumière où j'ai longtemps vécu." In a footnote to an essay in *Noces,* he criticizes Gide's attitude to the body, and says, "My friend Vincent, who is a cooper, and junior breast-stroke champion, has an even clearer view. He drinks when he is thirsty, if he desires a woman tries to go to bed with her, and would marry her if he loved her (this hasn't yet happened). Afterwards he says 'I feel better.' " Camus's affirmation of physical reality takes the form of a dismissal of anything that robs a man of his communion with the world. "I do not want to believe that death opens out into another life. For me it is a closed door . . . a horrible and dirty adventure. All the solutions that are offered to me try to rob man of the weight of his own life.

* It is interesting to note that D. H. Lawrence was temperamentally closer to Huxley and Sartre than to Hemingway or Camus. Although he lays such emphasis on physical affirmation, the effect of much of his later work — particularly *Lady Chatterley's Lover* — is of cantankerous disgust; only his very early work seems to be free from this attitude.

And watching the flight of the great birds in the sky at Djémila, it is exactly a certain weight in my life that I ask for and receive."

Here, then, is the simplest form of existentialism, a rejection of all "hereafters." Camus calls it "living without appeal." The world and man's life must be made to yield their own realities, without recourse to myth or "sacred" text.

The next step in Camus's development occurs in his novel *L'Etranger* and the "essay in the absurd," *Mythe de Sisyphe* (*The Myth of Sisyphus*). The proposition at the basis of *L'Etranger* could be summarized as "The world is a beast of a place" (in which the novel strongly resembles *A Farewell to Arms:* "They would get you in the end.") *Mythe de Sisyphe* compares man's position in the world with that of Sisyphus, condemned forever to roll a rock up a mountain and watch it roll down again — the symbol of utter futility. Yet he concludes: "One must imagine Sisyphus happy." At the end of *L'Etranger,* Meursault, who has been condemned to death for a crime of which he is not guilty, has a sudden vision of the utter indifference of the universe, and concludes, "I had been happy, and I was happy still." It is a gospel of complete inner-direction, that in spite of physical bondage, man is free and will always remain free. He may not know it, but his freedom is indestructible. When he knows it, as Meursault does in a sudden vision, he is happy as well as free, but it doesn't really matter whether he is happy or not; he is always free. *HE IS NOT TILL HE IS SELF-SECURED FROM ANY DELUSION DANGER*

But the absurdity of the world remains a terrible and hostile force. In *Le Malentendu,* a play, a man comes back to a country inn without telling his mother or sister

— who keep the inn — of his identity. They murder him in the night. The next day, when they find out (through his wife), they kill themselves. But the absurdity of their fate is only a tiny part of the "monstrous injustice that is done to man."

In his later work, Camus ceases to lay so much emphasis on the world's monstrous absurdity. In *La Peste,* he symbolizes man's position in the world in his story of a city trapped by plague; no one is allowed in or out. The final message of *La Peste* is of human solidarity.

Camus's next major work, *L'Homme Révolté (The Rebel),* caused a quarrel with Sartre, who had had nothing but praise for *L'Etranger* and *La Peste.* It is true that *L'Homme Révolté* can be construed as reactionary. It is an examination of various types of rebellion and a demonstration that they all end by becoming false to their original spirit. "It is a question of finding out whether innocence, the moment it begins to act, can avoid committing murder." The book should be read immediately after Whyte's *The Organization Man* (especially the chapters on literature), for it is a kind of handbook for aspiring rebels. Its main thesis is that the only kind of rebellion that does not end by contradicting itself is that of the man who retains his full integrity and power of choice. "The revolutionary mind . . . must . . . draw its inspiration from the only system of thought which is faithful to its origins: thought which recognizes limits." In this sentence, Camus has aligned himself with T. E. Hulme and T. S. Eliot as a supporter of classicism, and an opponent of romanticism.

For Sartre, who was at this time (1951) a declared communist sympathiser, this was a declaration of disagreement.

As a preacher of a vague notion of "freedom" and "choice," Sartre was open to a charge of romanticism. As a man who had committed himself to the communist ideology, he was open to an accusation of compromise. As a writer who had drawn a sympathetic portrait of a would-be dictator who regards the end as more important than the means (Hoeder in *Les Mains Sales*), he was open to an accusation of totalitarianism. *Les Temps Modernes* accordingly attacked Camus as a reactionary, condemning his "ivory tower" attitude, and a correspondence between Sartre and Camus ensued, which generated more heat than light.

The original review of the book was by François Jeanson, who denounced it as insidious and accused Camus of providing the forces of reaction with a weapon. Camus replied in a scathing and irritated letter to "the editor of *Les Temps Modernes*," and this provoked a reply from both Jeanson and Sartre. In the course of the correspondence, certain fundamental differences became quite clear: for instance, that Camus conceives himself primarily as an *influence,* while Sartre is more concerned with constructing a doctrine that will turn the potential energy of his ideas into kinetic energy, a *force.* Sartre declared that his concern is with present injustice, not with theorizing about the impossibility of remedying injustice. Jeanson stated that for Camus the problem of God is of more concern than the problem of man. Camus was accused of distorting history for his own purposes and of having an active dislike of history. (This allegation was based on a passage in Camus's *Lettres à un Ami Allemand,* in which he complains that the war has torn him away from his metaphysical conflicts and forced him to take part in the boring

and banal struggles of mankind.) Camus's replies are
mainly a defense of his arguments in *L'Homme Révolté*
and a further attack on Marxism; he accuses Sartre and
Jeanson of equating critical intelligence with reaction.
Sartre's objection to these replies could be summarized:
"I agree with most of your accusations against communism.
The fact remains that something must be done about injustice, and your book gives lazy people an excuse for not
doing anything." Sartre summed up the whole argument:
"Many things brought us together, few separated us, but
even those few were too many."

Camus's next two important volumes deepen his position
without enlarging it. His stories in *L'Exil et le Royaume*
(*Exile and the Kingdom*) all deal, in different ways, with
people who feel themselves to be spiritual exiles and who
search for some way out of their exile, towards some "kingdom." One of the stories, "The Guest," seems to be a
return to the old theme that "the world is a beast," the
absurdity and injustice of life. Another deals with a famous
painter who lets too many hangers-on waste his time and
finally has to retreat into solitude. When he falls ill, a
single word is found scrawled on his canvas, which might
be either "solitary" or "solidarity" — Camus's implication being that they are the same thing, that an artist can
best serve the community by remaining solitary. Perhaps
the most interesting story in the collection is "The Woman
Taken in Adultery," a strangely D. H. Lawrence-like work
in which a middle-aged married woman has an experience
of mystical marriage with the earth in the North African
night. Together with the end of *L'Etranger* and the passage I have cited about the "great birds in the sky at

Djémila," it is a statement of Camus's positive belief, a sort of mysticism.

The novel *La Chute* (*The Fall*) is certainly Camus's most important work to date, although it is barely a hundred pages long. It is a study in bad faith and the attempt to transcend it. Jean-Baptiste Clamence begins life as a lawyer, well known for his charities and his championship of the oppressed. Camus portrays him as a man who is an ideal member of society, generous, good-natured, "well adjusted." Then he pulls the lever, and reveals that Clamence's altruism is a form of self-deception; he is a do-gooder because it makes him feel good on a purely personal level. Society may approve of him, but Clamence's greatest moment occurs when his own conscience ceases to do so. This happens when he is crossing a bridge and hears a woman throw herself into the water. It is late at night, and he hurries on, preferring not to retrace his steps and make futile gestures to save her. For a while he can rationalize his failure to attempt a rescue, but the real reason forces itself on him: his altruism was not a real love of human beings, but a love of being regarded as an altruist. He throws up his practice and goes to Amsterdam, to become a kind of Ancient Mariner, sitting in a café, getting into conversation with compatriots, and trying to give them the same insight into their own self-deceptions. He regards life as wholly composed of types of self-deception and absurdity.

Camus's attitude towards Clamence is not wholly one of approval. He has said, in conversations, that Clamence is a typical French left-wing intellectual, capable of criticizing everybody and everything in the world (including

[handwritten marginalia:] IS NOT THIS ENOUGH AS A GOOD FEELING TO DO GOOD! AS LONG AS HE IS DOING IT NO MATTER OF THE ORIGIN OF THE MOTIVE!

BUT HE IS DO-GOODER
DO-GOODER
WHAT ELSE
IS THERE

himself) but not capable of doing much else besides talk. Nevertheless, Clamence demonstrates effectively Camus's most important assertion: that being a "good member of society" is not enough. Camus keeps returning to the individual. In this, he is a true existentialist — in rejecting all attempts to fit the individual into some larger social pattern.

46   In many ways, Camus is a more interesting figure than Sartre, although his range as a writer is narrower. At the age of forty-six (he was born in 1913) he has achieved in France a curious eminence that is based entirely upon his recognized integrity. His influence among the younger generation of French intellectuals might well be compared to that of T. S. Eliot in England before he became an Anglican. In some way, he is felt to typify the dilemma of the average Frenchman of intelligence. His position is enviable, for without having compromised himself, without joining any religious or political group, he has succeeded in becoming a figurehead in French intellectual life. He has also avoided the greatest danger of being "uncommitted": being admired by a clique, and generally ignored (in the manner of a Ronald Firbank or L. H. Myers).

And yet, like Sartre, Camus has certain clearly defined limitations. It is extremely difficult to see how he can maneuver his existentialism out of the impasse it seems to have reached. (A recent book on him speculated whether his next move might not be to join the Catholic church, but this is hardly likely.)

His limitations have very little in common with Sartre's. While Sartre has devoted most of his energy during the past ten years to politics, Camus has continued to explore the basic problems of existentialism. (On one occasion, he spoke of his main preoccupation — somewhat rhetorically — as his "quarrel with God.") Sartre has preferred to concentrate on the position of the worker in modern Europe; Camus is more interested in the position of man in the universe. In this, he has remained closer to the spirit of existentialism than Sartre. His readers have come to accept that his "solution," when and if it comes, will be some individual vision, some reconciling insight into the condition of man. Yet although Camus has been deeply influenced by Dostoevsky, he seems to lack the temperament that can reach towards mystical insights, the vision that compensates an Alyosha Karamazov for the nihilism of Ivan. Camus's position is not unlike Ivan's. He is keenly aware of human suffering, of the world's hostile absurdity; like Ivan, he is an atheist; like Ivan, he loves life in spite of the absurdity. Even though Camus has reconciled himself to his own vision of absurdity, although his final position is one of affirmation, he makes on the reader the impression of being a negative writer, negative in spite of his intention. Compared with most American (and English) writers, he has achieved complete inner-direction; his writing has a subjective integrity with which very few of his contemporaries can compare. But there is still a strong element of the cult of the ordinary chap in him. He himself would undoubtedly acknowledge this, and insist that it is necessarily so. But the fact that it is a self-imposed limitation does not make it any the less a limitation.

In spite of the criticisms that may be leveled against them, both Sartre and Camus have achieved remarkable results, and their complete seriousness has never been in question. Their conclusions may be regarded as doubtful, but the psychological method of analysis, perfected by them both, will remain an invaluable instrument for existential thinkers in the future.

Conclusion

The problem that Riesman and Whyte explore at such length is fundamentally the same problem that Sartre and Camus have attacked. For instance, Riesman, writing of the other-directed businessman, says: "Obliged to conciliate or manipulate a variety of people, the other-directed person handles all men as customers who are always right; but he must do this with the uneasy realization that . . . some are more right than others. . . . [Thus] the other-directed person tends to become merely his succession of roles and encounters and *hence to doubt who he is or where he is going*" (my italics). This could hardly be plainer. Hell is other people. Riesman is describing inauthentic existence. All Sartre's analyses of inauthentic existence are really analyses of other-direction. When Electra in *Les Mouches* allows Zeus to persuade her to repent, she is being other-directed. And Sartre's insistence upon the act of choice is echoed by Whyte when he advises the organization man to think for himself and defy the boss.

It could be said, then, that Sartre and Camus have spent the past twenty years trying to propound answers to the same problems that Riesman and Whyte have more recently analyzed. Moreover, the American sociologists and the French thinkers have arrived at these statements by completely different routes. Riesman makes it clear that he considers the spread of other-direction to be due to the switch of emphasis in American economic life from production to consumption. Sartre and Camus know that the roots of existentialism can be traced back for at least a century and a half. And yet all four are ultimately concerned with the loss of autonomy in modern man. Riesman, like Camus, has no practical solutions to offer. Whyte, like Sartre, propounds a limited solution: he urges the organization man to make an act of choice, to refuse to be treated like a package of consumer goods.

The existential method has proved itself a more subtle instrument of analysis of other-direction than the sociological method (although it is not, for this reason, wholly superior). To what extent, then, can existentialism offer a solution to the problems of "the lonely crowd"?

The question bristles with difficulties. And the first of these is the lack of *positive* content in French existentialism. Existentialism began as a revolt (against Hegel), and a revolt is essentially negative. It has continued as an analysis of human psychology and the human situation. But the analysis halts before it reaches the point of synthesis. Is it possible for existentialism to become something more positive?

Part Five

The Stature of Man

FROM the considerations of the last part, one point emerges with undeniable clarity; the responsibility of the writer in our time. His responsibility is heavier than that of the politicians or the church, for what is in question is a *revolution in thought*, not a five-year plan or a recipe for "getting right with God." Man in the twentieth century suffers from an insignificance neurosis, which can only be attacked from inside. Riesman puts his finger on it when he says, "It is not only that [the other-directed man] withdraws emotional allegiance from a political scene that strikes him as too complex and too unmanageable — *it strikes him so in part precisely because he has withdrawn*" (my italics). If it is a mental attitude that has created the problem, then it will be a change of attitude that will be the first step in solving it.

"Insignificance" is a literary trend that can be combated. Arthur Miller indicated that he considered a "heroic" revolt might produce a new romanticism, a defeat for realism. This only demonstrates that for Miller the word "heroic" means what it meant for Cervantes: ranting and posturing. This is a negative view. The insignificance fallacy will not be destroyed by a mere desire to create characters who are not creatures of their environment. Only a positive conviction can hope to do it. This requires a careful definition of the concept of the heroic. And this, in turn, requires an advance beyond the existentialism of Sartre and Camus.

Three Types of Commitment

Before considering the more complex issues, the recurring question of commitment deserves to be examined.

There are three obvious ways in which a writer can be committed to take social action, and three possible motives:

1. Self-interest. The writer is committed to civilization, and therefore to world peace, because he writes for a civilization, and his aim is to add something to civilized values.

2. Dislike of cruelty. This is an instinctive response in anyone who is aware of himself as a member of society, and is an outcome of the ability to identify with other people. The degree to which a man may feel committed to oppose cruelty depends upon two factors: his imagination, and the energy he has to spare from his own internal struggles.

3. Desire for fuller self-expression. For men of a certain temperament — Shaw and Sartre are examples — writing is not finally a completely satisfying means of self-expression. Sartre is obsessed by the idea that philosophy should lead to action.

The first of these seems to me to be the most important.

To be a thinking, responsive human being means to realize that even a Trappist monk owes his ability to save himself to the fact that he has been born into a human society and taught modes of self-expression. In the mid-twentieth century, all values are threatened by the possibility of the destruction of civilization. Every issue that constitutes a threat to peace — whether immediate or indirect — demands an attitude of commitment. For this reason, issues like the Suez crisis, the occupation of Cyprus, the South Africa treason trials, the hydrogen bomb tests demand a definite attitude. (The writer should not underestimate his possible influence in these matters. Alexander Werth states that the attitude of *Les Temps Modernes* helped to discourage the Americans from launching a preventive anti-Soviet crusade at the time of the witch hunts.) And if the writer is committed to preserving peace, he is also committed to conserving the values of peace in times of crisis, to not allowing himself to be swayed by popular emotions, to resisting the forces that blur our language. (Again, *Les Temps Modernes* has been disinterested in attacking Russia and the West; Sartre has frequently declared that he will not allow particular instances — the concentration camps, the Hungarian rising — to make him anti-Russian, although he has given full prominence to Russian, as well as American, abuses in his magazine.)

The second type of commitment — dislike of cruelty — is certainly of immense importance, but it is so deeply ingrained in most civilized men (or we are to hope it is) as to need no underlining. Here again, the writer's role can be of great importance. The recent campaign against capital punishment is an example. (Camus has written a long article opposing capital punishment, which has had considerable impact in France.) *

The third type of commitment requires no elaboration. But it throws into relief another important aspect of this question. Committed writers often speak as if it were a form of cowardice to be uncommitted. They are ignoring the most important fact about any kind of creation: that it originates on a level below the "social personality." The ideally mature creator may be able to act and create out of the same impulse, without doing violence to either. But for less mature artists — and this covers ninety-nine per cent of the species — there is a problem of self-division: action is essentially the opposite of creation, and the social personality must be balanced in such a way as to give the maximum freedom to the creative drives. It is no use telling a subjective young poet that he *ought* to be taking part in marches to oppose the H-bomb tests. The probable result will be to make him say, "To hell with the tests; I'm a poet, not a politician." He says this not because he ultimately means it but because it is a response to the bludgeon tactics of people who lack the subtlety to realize that all men are necessarily self-divided. (This, of course, forms a powerful argument against the state control of artists practiced in the Soviet Union.)

But the final point about commitment leads directly to

* In the autumn of 1958, it was reported in the Sunday newspapers that a Negro was to be hanged in one of the Southern states of America for the theft of a few dollars; his execution was to occur during the following week. Within a matter of days, there was a world-wide protest that finally secured a reprieve. In this case, the flagrant unfairness of the sentence aroused people to protest. But such encouraging responses are not frequent; most people feel that their protest would have no effect anyway. In that case, the responsibility is left in the hands of a minority who are not diffident about the importance of what they have to say.

the central problem of existentialism. For Sartre, commitment means action. *But great art is action.* This is to say
that the Soviet critics who attacked Joyce's *Ulysses* for
having no message for he worker were ignoring the fact
that an artist's intensity cannot be turned on and off like
a tap. Great action, like great art, rises from a subpersonal
level. But ordinary action, the uninspired variety, is "of
the personality." The artist who becomes too obsessed with
the idea of translating art into action will become a
mediocre artist. This, perhaps, explains why Sartre's *Les
Chemins de la Liberté* is an artistic failure in comparison
with *Ulysses* or *Crime and Punishment.* (Sartre dislikes
Flaubert because of the contempt the latter felt for the
working classes; he also seems to feel that Baudelaire ought
to have allied himself with the working-class movement
instead of writing *Les Fleurs du Mal.*)

Towards a New Existentialism

This points to one of the main causes of the failure of
French existentialism. It has failed to place sufficient
emphasis on the creative drives. It deifies the ordinary at
the expense of the extraordinary. One might adapt Shaw's
comment on Shakespeare, and say that it understands
human weakness without understanding human strength.

Why are Sartre and Camus so preoccupied with the
"ordinary man"? It could be due to the fact that both
came to maturity as writers during the rise of Nazism, that
both worked in the resistance in occupied France, that
Sartre was interned in Germany at one stage. For five years
"freedom" meant freedom from the Nazis; such an experience can be expected to leave a permanent bias. This

is both a weakness and a strength; a weakness for the reasons I have discussed, a strength because it endowed them with a formidable single-mindedness.*

It can be said of existentialism that it has rescued religious concepts from the limbo of superstitions. Sartre's *mauvaise foi,* Heidegger's "inauthentic existence" are in practice identical with pride and sin. The final recrudescence of religion in the nineteenth century had been also its complete betrayal by language: the popular church movements, the Theosophical Society, the Christian Scientists, all helped to blur and discredit religious concepts. To the existentialists belongs the credit of restoring to these concepts the precision they possess in the work of Pascal or Saint Augustine.

But pride, sin, and delusion are the negative part of religion. The positive part has not experienced the same rehabilitation. It is true that Sartre speaks of "salvation," but his use of the word commands no conviction.

The problem, then, will be to create a new positive existentialism. It would not be accurate to say that this would have to begin where Sartre and Camus left off, for both have been committed for some time to the direction that appears to have led to an impasse; a new existentialism would have to begin further back, utilizing only their psychological method.

An example might clarify this point. The question at issue is of the positive and negative aspects of existentialism: these are exemplified in D. H. Lawrence's story, "The

---

* This became apparent to me when I discussed Camus's philosophy with him in Paris, and questioned him on his distrust of all "visionary" or religious solutions. He indicated a Parisian teddy boy who was slouching past the window, and commented: "Salvation for me must be also salvation for him."

Man Who Died." The story falls into two parts. In the first, Jesus rises from the tomb, exhausted and shattered by his experience, robbed of the moral energy that led him to preach. In this state, his activities in the past seem futile, inspired by delusion and egoism. This is the typical existential attack on idealism; Lawrence is accusing Jesus of robbing life of its real values by imposing a set of ideal values on it. In this respect, the first part of the story corresponds quite precisely with Camus's *La Chute,* or Sartre's *La Nausée.* It shows the breakdown of a man's belief in his values.

But Lawrence goes further. Having demolished these ideal values (to his own satisfaction), he goes on to make the attempt to replace them with real values. It goes without saying that these involve sex. In the first part of the story, Jesus has seen a cock strutting among its hens and is struck by the fact that this is the law of life: will to power and propagation. In the second part, he experiences this himself when he comes to an Egyptian temple in the wilderness and has sex with a priestess of Isis. (This is the part of the story that was denounced as blasphemous on its publication.) This restores his contact with life and turns him into a mystical worshiper of the life-force.

Most readers will suspect that Lawrence achieved this demonstration at the expense of a certain distortion of the values concerned. But this, although it may invalidate the argument in the last analysis, leaves its logical beauty unaffected. In its way, the story has the perfection of a geometrical theorem; it moves inevitably from a critical existentialism to a visionary and positive existentialism. No work of Sartre or Camus makes any attempt to reach this second stage. Sartre's "L'Enfance d'un Chef" shows

Lucien Fleurier losing all integrity in self-deception; only by implication is it positive. Camus's *La Peste* ends with a stoical gesture of endurance: "The problems may be insoluble, but human beings have one another." No matter how suspect Lawrence's solution may be, no matter how much he may have distorted the views he wishes to attack, he has at least laid down a solution with no attempt at evasion.

It is worth noting that Lawrence's method is the purest kind of existentialism. It is the most basic human response to life that he keeps referring to; nothing more grandiose is acceptable. He is an intuitive Blakeian; his aim is to "renew the fiery joy, and burst the stony roof" (of idealism and intellectualism). But this Blakeian approach led him into a rejection of all commitment; he insisted on the importance of conflict, the clash of wills. In politics, his ideas were based firmly on the dictator principle (although this was mainly because he envisaged himself as the dictator). This needs emphasizing because Lawrence was a better existentialist than Sartre or Camus; he stuck closer to first principles, and relied completely on intuition. There is no point in disguising the fact that positive existentialism *can* steer very close to fascism. This will require further analysis.

Existentialism and the Hero

How far can critical analysis hope to create a new existentialism? Its value is obviously limited to clearing the ground. The actual edifice must be the work of poets and novelists.

This is the first major point of disagreement with Sartre.

With some justification, he feels that philosophizing and criticizing are "just talk"; as an existentialist, he has no intention of being satisfied with talk. But his next step is more dubious; he believes that *therefore* a philosophy will prove its sincerity by striving continually to ally itself with action. In this, his attitude comes close to that of another existential thinker, Wittgenstein, who believed that language can only express things that are not worth expressing and that a point comes when the philosopher has to "be silent." This is to ignore the fact that great literature is always expressing the inexpressible, since it has the same power as great music and painting to appeal directly to the vital intuitions. The results of Sartre's belief can be seen in his writing. *La Nausée* was written before he developed his views on commitment, and it has passages of extraordinary power and beauty; the later novels are competent, but pedestrian. It is a fallacy to believe that action can get closer to life than writing. The aim of philosophy is depth and vital intensity. Political action *could* give philosophy this added dimension; it could also produce total confusion.

At this point, the problem links up with the main subject of this essay, the hero. The aim of the new existentialism is identical with that of the hero and the inner-directed man: to be reconnected with the vital impulses and the sense of purpose. The old hero was simply the man who had defeated most enemies, rescued most damsels, overcome the most obstacles in his search for the Grail. But Faust had stumbled on the solution for the new hero, when the Easter bells revealed to him that his salvation lay in a *deepening of internal experience*. Unfortunately, he failed to grasp the meaning of the insight. It remains a completely unexplored direction in literature (if Proust's experiment is excepted).

It will be pointed out that a book about what goes on inside a man's mind might be rather a bore. In fact, this constitutes one of the great challenges of a new existentialism. Mental processes are usually stimulated and paralleled by physical experiences; the writer who finally solves the problem will be able to add another chapter to James' classic treatise on the art of the novel.

The basis of a new existentialism must be an understanding of the nature of action. A man might go through a whole series of actions with a sense of total unreality; in that case, he cannot be said to have acted. In the same way, a man who has been to bed with a hundred girls would not necessarily have known deeper sexual experience than an imaginative boy who is having his first love affair.

This is only to say that the fundamental experience of existentialism is the sense of being reconnected to reality. Lawrence recognized the power of the sexual act to bring this about; he was mistaken in supposing that it was the only way. A very slight acquaintance with Blake or Traherne, or even Proust, is enough to confirm this point.*

The writers of England and America have a slight advantage over their continental colleagues in possessing a native tradition of positive existentialism. It is a tradition of *affirmative and irrational mysticism* that can be found in Blake, Whitman, Yeats, Joyce, and Shaw, as well as in a host of lesser figures. In twentieth-century American literature, it can be found in Scott Fitzgerald, Thomas Wolfe, and Jack Kerouac; in England in Chesterton, Belloc, and Rupert Brooke. Kerouac's *On the Road* fur-

* Lawrence dismisses Proust as "effete" in *Lady Chatterley's Lover.*

nishes an interesting example; it is full of Whitmanesque dithyrambs on the size and variety of America, and outbursts of sheer joy at being alive. In this, Kerouac may have been influenced by Wolfe's *Of Time and the River* and Fitzgerald's *This Side of Paradise*. Fitzgerald was certainly influenced by the mystical optimism of Chesterton and Belloc. It is a mood that seems foreign to French and German writers (Nietzsche being the sole exception I can bring to mind).

It might be objected that many of the writers I cite have (or had) the advantage of youth; the later work of Wolfe and Fitzgerald has pessimistic overtones. But this is no final argument against irrational mysticism. Whitman, Blake, and Chesterton maintained their attitude into old age. Yeats' *Last Poems* provide many examples; the poems "Lapis Lazuli" and "Under Ben Bulben," and the lines from "The Gyres":

> *Out of cavern comes a voice,*
> *And all it knows is that one word "Rejoice!"*

The Absurd Man

Can this mysticism be placed upon a firm basis of existential philosophy? The task would require a critique of negative existentialism that is beyond the scope of this essay. But the direction of such a critique might be indicated briefly.

The existentialism of Sartre and Camus fails to take full account of the dualism of man. Their heroes are brought to earth by reality. The role of reality is rather like that of a kick in the stomach. Reality presses on them like an enemy; concepts are as useless as a broadsword in close combat. It is too close; it presses and stifles. The hero has to learn that he has no appeal. He must come to terms with this enemy within his gates. It is no use looking to religion or human companionship; only a certain stoicism and determination can be of any use.

But in fact, man never has to face *anything* as finally as that. No matter what realities he has to face, a part of him remains detached. Upon this rests our optimism and strength. If there is any reality that must be faced without alternative, then man is damned. His hope lies in his ultimate and indestructible freedom, a freedom that implies that he always has the choice of realities because *he is* the final reality.

This is the basis of all true mysticism. Because it denies our realities, it is absurd. But its absurdity is not Camus's "malicious absurdity"; Chesterton came closer to it when he spoke of "absurd good news."

For this reason, the hero can be defined as *the absurd man*. In effect, he is the man who can perform a conjuring trick by which he empties his hands *and still possesses everything*. If he does not believe in himself sufficiently to direct his desire towards the unattainable, he is no hero. When Auden rephrased Yeats' lines:

> *Across the tohu bohu comes a voice*
> *Uttering an absurd command: "Rejoice!"*

he had caught the essence of mystical optimism. Captain Ahab is the great absurd hero; he has no rivals. (It is unfortunate that Chesterton, who understood the spirit of absurdity so well, never embodied it in any single major work.)

*POSSIBILITY OF CONINUINS TO LIVE HAPPY
WITH A SKILL GIVES ONE HOW TO BE IMPORTANT
REGARDLESS
WHY NOT FIND A JOB FOR OR LIVING
+ PAINTING
MYSTICAL
OPTIMISIM ?
MEANING
LIVING
BEYOND
REALITY
MYTA—
PHISICAL
CULTISISM*

In modern English writing, I know of only one attempt to convey this absurd affirmation: Joyce Cary's novel, *The Horse's Mouth*. It deals with a sixty-seven-year-old painter who lives in a broken-down shack at the side of the river in East London. Although he has every reason to be tired of life — being penniless, toothless, and practically friendless — he seems to spend most of his time in visionary ecstasies. The following is a typical example:

" 'Up with you,' said Coker, pushing me on the bus, and planting me between a navvy smelling like an old stable and an old woman with a sore nose and a basket full of pig's food.

*For every generated body in its inward form
Is a garden of delight and a building of magnificence
Built by the sons of Los."*

This is the way in which Cary gains most of his effects; contrasting Jimson's attitude with his thoughts (helped out with liberal quotations from Blake). And Jimson's last speech in the novel summarizes its mood:

The angel, in fact, that presided at my birth—her name was old mother Groper or something like that—village midwife. Worn-out tart from the sailor's knocking shop. Sad little creature born of joy and mirth. Though I must admit that poor Papa was so distracted with debt and misery that I daresay he didn't know what he was doing. And poor Mamma, yes, she was glad to give him what she could, if it didn't cost anything and didn't wear out the family clothes. . . . Go love without the help of anything on earth. . . . A man is more independent that way, when he doesn't expect anything for himself. *HOW DOES HE MAKE LIVING FOR HIMSELF !*

It will be seen that the actual *content* of the passage is Dostoevskian: human misery and injustice contrasted with a sense of visionary affirmation; many passages from *Crime and Punishment, The Devils, The Brothers Karamazov* could be cited as parallels. But Cary's tone is completely different; there is an attempt to see the greatness and misery simultaneously. This is not always successful; the mysticism often fails to blend with the Rabelaisian humor, and the result is an effect of strain and clumsiness. Moreover, Jimson fails to convince as a "man of genius"; some of his transitions from earthy humor to visionary ecstasy seem labored. The short, terse sentences are reminiscent of Joyce's, but their flow is clogged by constant attempts to be funny. To be really convincing, Jimson should convey an impression of unreflective sincerity; instead, he often sounds like a third-rate comedian.

The Horse's Mouth is not, finally, a successful novel, but it is the only attempt I know to present man's "two-fold vision" in every aspect of his life. Jimson is an embodiment of Rilke's idea of *dennoch preisen,* "praising in spite of." Joyce had brushed past the theme in *Ulysses,* where Stephen walks along the beach and quotes fragments of Blake and Boehme ("Signature of all things I am here to read" and "Am I walking into Eternity along Sandymount Strand"). Certain phrases in the last section also suggest a mystical intent, while whole passages in *Finnegans Wake* seem to express a pure affirmation. These occasional attempts of Joyce are more convincing than Cary's; their emotional drive is unhampered by facetiousness. But it is difficult to see how the problem might be ultimately solved; how the two-fold vision could be presented as seriously as in Joyce and as fully as in *The Horse's Mouth.*

To some extent, the work of Alain Robbe-Grillet and his disciples represents a protest against the unheroic premise. Robbe-Grillet is the *avant-garde* novelist who describes objects at such extraordinary length. In an article, "A Fresh Start for Fiction," in the *Evergreen Review* (No. 3), he explains his dislike of the way in which writers treat objects as mere background material and imbue them with their emotions. A landscape becomes "soothing," a broken tree "menacing," and so on. Robbe-Grillet attempts to bring objects to the foreground in his work; the actions of his characters take place among an infinitely real and obtrusively solid set of objects. In practice, of course, his everlasting descriptions slow down his work and rob the action of its impact. But the theory behind it has something in common with the idea which Blake expressed in his lines:

> *How do you know but every bird that cuts the airy way,*
> *Is an immense world of delight, closed to your senses five?*

Blake is protesting against the way in which we allow things to become familiar until we take them for granted. The world becomes narrow, boring, personal. But Blake insists on an infinite mystical reality concealed behind the façade of the everyday, and believes that it is the artist's function to express it. Robbe-Grillet rejects the familiarity of objects but has no vision of their mystical strangeness. Like the Angries and the Beats, his revolt stops halfway.

A God or a Worm?

The central preoccupation of existentialism can be defined in one phrase: the stature of man. Is he a god or a worm?

Modern literature takes the latter view. This is not because all modern writers are unaware of the alternative. Even Sartre's Roquentin has strange godlike moods. But the tendency of the age has been to emphasize the insignificance of man, his misery and weakness. It is all a question of emphasis. In most cases, there is no question of the writer's conviction. He follows the trend of the age. William James observed that the religious man is not necessarily the man who has had most religious experience; he is the man who makes his religious experiences his *center of gravity*. The same is true of the writer. He can affirm or deny, according to an act of will. And he is determined by that act of will, not by "the facts." There are no facts, only experiences of the facts that are determined by the individual's attitude. Sartre's insistence on man's fundamental freedom is only a restatement of the religious concept of faith, and the "faith" is another name for belief in the absurd.

Neither is it true to assert that the ages of faith are past and that we live in an age of skepticism or defeat. The age is an abstraction; only the individuals who make it are real. Man's experience of himself is at all times a simultaneous experience of greatness and misery, god and worm. He is free to give primacy to either of these experiences. Like a compass, he is pivoted between acceptance of defeat or belief in the absurd. Whichever he chooses can determine his existence and, ultimately, his age.

The acceptance of this view could affect the writer in certain obvious ways. The novelist or playwright who creates characters who are slaves of their environment does so because he accepts their predicament as his own. The conscious rejection of the unheroic hypothesis, the in-

significance premise, might produce some interesting results. It might reveal that the influence of the writer on
society is actually greater than the influence society is
supposed to have on the writer. If this were established,
it would reveal that all writers are committed whether
they know it or not, committed up to the hilt in determin-
ing the attitudes of the society they live in.

In the second part of this essay, I criticized certain
American writers for lacking an awareness of "man as an
evolving spiritual being." The phrase goes to the heart
of the hero problem. It has been universally taken for
granted that inner-direction is preferable to other-direction
(except, perhaps, in the writings of certain Soviet pundits).
But *why* should this be so? What is the ultimate justification of inner-direction? Unless a phrase like "man as an
evolving spiritual being" can be given precise signification,
inner-direction *cannot* be justified; it can only be taken for
granted. A new existentialism can only be built upon the
psychological concept of purpose, but "inner-direction" itself is not a purpose; it is only a means.

It is self-evident that any psychology I appeal to will
be, of necessity, my own psychology; that is, my own observations of my psychological responses to such experiences
as the nausea, vision, self-deception, and so forth. If I
find the psychology of Sartre and Camus inadequate, it
is not because I challenge their conclusions in the way
that one scientist might challenge the conclusions of another, but because their final picture of the world does not
correspond to my own intuitive perception of it. But
the attempt to present this perception as existential
thought demands that I express it in the same language,
using the same concepts, as Sartre and Camus.

Like religion, existentialism begins from the concept of the fallen man — that is, of man's feeling of the world's hostile strangeness. This is Sartre's "nausea."

When I inquire into my own experience of nausea, I discover that it is closely connected with a great number of other terms: "unreality," "boredom," "futility," "frustration." In the journal I kept from the age of sixteen, these were the terms that expressed my sense of alienation.

It happens often that after a long period of boredom, the sense of purpose has been so far submerged that the *physical actuality* of the world becomes a denial of meaning. Yeats expressed the nausea in that poem called "The Circus Animals' Desertion," where he spoke of his early romantic idealism as a ladder and ended:

> *Now that my ladder's gone,*
> *I must lie down where all the ladders start,*
> *In the foul rag and bone shop of the heart.*

On my first reading of *Ulysses,* these lines of Yeats seemed to express its whole meaning.

In a sense, Sartre is right: the nausea is the ultimate reality. But men live on two planes at once; no ultimate can negate man's freedom. Sartre and Camus accept this to some extent (as many "unheroic" writers do: William Faulkner, for instance). But they are mainly aware of the "rag and bone shop"; their vision of freedom is, in comparison, distant and nostalgic. This leads to a neo-stoic position. No doubt these writers would object (quite understandably) that this is the way they see the world. And yet once it is established that the question is one of the balance between freedom and necessity (nausea), it becomes possible to reply that many other writers, Blake

among them, have possessed a vision of the world in which
there is a far higher percentage of freedom.

In the final analysis, the nausea is the fallacy of insignificance. It is expressed in Eliot's lines:

> *and leave me sitting, pen in hand . . .*
> *Not knowing what to feel, or if I understand.*

This feeling is existential; it refuses to put an interpretation on the world.

But the point that is being forgotten is that an ignorance
of meaning is not the same thing as a belief in meaningless-
ness. It may be bad faith to transform the surface of reality
with unverifiable beliefs of the Hegel type, but the attitude
of perpetual and urgent questioning is in itself a transfor-
mation. A Roquentin suffering from nausea is also suffering from boredom and his own littleness. A Pascal torn
between the greatness and the misery of man, a Van Gogh
who never ceases to be simultaneously aware of ultimate
agony and ultimate ecstasy, has already achieved a greater
stature than Roquentin by an intensity of questioning.
They may suffer from exhaustion, but never from the self-
contempt that comes from inaction. The existentialism of
Sartre or Camus lacks this final urgency of interrogation
and consequently lacks a dimension of freedom. To speak
of an impasse is to give the wrong impression, for it
suggests a logical cul-de-sac. It would be more accurate to
speak of a rocket that stops for lack of fuel. The fuel for
all existential thinkers must be that Dostoevskian passion
for measuring the paradoxes of the human condition;
symbolically, it sees man suspended in a void between
heaven and hell, god and worm. Sartre's preoccupation

with politics, Camus's desire to reduce the paradox to the language of the teddy boy rob their interrogation of motive power.

I stated at one stage in this essay that the hero's problem is to turn inward, *and then outward again*. The above paragraphs provide a basis on which to expand this conception. The purpose of turning inward is to discover one's freedom. All men are supplied by a power house of will and subconscious drive, but very few are aware of anything but the need to keep alive. It is hardly surprising that most men think of their motives in terms of everyday necessities. Considered from this point of view, all life is seen as an ascending hierarchy of mechanisms, beginning with the need to eat and breathe, and developing to levels of ambition, self-assertion (will to power), and so on. This is to hold the problem upside down, but it makes very little difference so long as men are committed to some objective purpose. It is also the unheroic hypothesis. But confronted by any man with an inborn sense of purpose, it appears as nausea, a denial of life and freedom. The highest compliment Shakespeare's Antony could pay Brutus was: "This was a man." Nietzsche or Sartre would retort that only insofar as he was unaware of his freedom was he a man; insofar as he was free, he was not anything but potentiality of will and purpose.

But the sense of purpose is nothing without a goal. And this is where French existentialism flags. For although Sartre has maneuvered himself out of the extreme position of total nausea and life rejection, he has never learned to speak authoritatively of human purpose. He remains limited to the particularity of men and history, too cautious to pass beyond these to the notion of life itself. Camus asks: "Why do men not commit suicide?" and answers: "Because of an irrational urge to live." But he builds no artistic edifice on that recognition; one suspects that he feels a certain mortification at being forced to use the word "irrational" and wishes it could be avoided.

To escape these limitations, it is necessary to base existential thought on the foundations of the absurd, the irrational, the mystical. To say that men are *not* men, but raw, unqualified freedom, is to assert that the life urge can never be justified by reasons. Adversity can concentrate it to a point of ecstasy; threatened extinction can reveal it as independent of all human values. This is a reassertion of a kind of Platonic idealism; the love of life is not a love of any aspect of living, but a pure need, beyond objects. It is expressed concisely in Blake's line, "Go, love without the help of anything on earth." Both Sartre and Heidegger have observed that life can be lived most intensely in the face of death, but neither has recognized that the sense of death is only an extension of life, and *that a sense of purpose would be a still further extension*. This, I believe, is the reason for the thin and unsatisfying tone of Sartre's views on commitment.

Conclusion

I would summarize my conclusions as follows:

The fallacy of insignificance can be combated on the writer's front by a deliberate attempt to replace worn-out religious and cultural concepts with a new existentialism.

This existentialism must make the fullest use of the

invaluable work of thinkers like Kierkegaard, Heidegger, Sartre, and Camus, but its chief task is to break beyond their limitations.

I envisage the new existentialism as a mystical revolt, based upon recognition of the irrational urge that underlies man's conscious reason. The writer's task is to try to make the "noise of the power house" audible.

For this reason, I regard Blake and Shaw as seminal figures, in that both were permanently aware of the power house. Their rationalizations of it are less important (Blake's "Jerusalem," Shaw's "vortex of pure intellect," superman, and so forth). What matters is that they recognized the need to give life an additional dimension of purpose.

The existential revolt could take place on two levels: the philosophical, and the creative. On the first level, it might produce its own textbooks of irrational philosophy to take up the problem where Sartre left it in *L'Être et le Néant,* Heidegger in *Sein und Zeit,* Camus in *L'Homme Révolté.* On the creative level, it would be a revolt against the unheroic premise, the attempt to create heroes who possess a vision that extends beyond the particularities of environment. This does not necessarily mean a hero who carries a copy of *Man and Superman* in his pocket, but it means heroes who are closer in conception to Stendhal's Sorel, Balzac's Rastignac, Braine's Joe Lampton, Hopkins' Plowart. It is even conceivable that new, realistic Fausts, Zarathustras, Ahabs might grow out of it.

Ultimately, the hero is the man who lives constantly out of a sense of his own freedom; his commitment to the world is nourished by his inwardness, and his inwardness is constantly strengthened through being reflected back from society. Such a man would recognize all life as sacred, as all is involved in the same struggle towards expression of its freedom.

The artist who hopes to create the existential hero will inevitably find himself in opposition to many modern trends. All philosophies of materialism promote the insignificance fallacy. Great efforts of creation are made only by men who believe in their will and the importance of effort. Marxian materialism and Freudian psychology are excuses for laziness. Shaw's Saint Joan remarked: "Minding your own business is like minding your own body — it's the shortest way to make yourself sick." The same might be said of minding your own mind, or the way in which you've been conditioned by the economic structure of society.

Too many aspects of modern culture provide this excuse for laziness and hypochondria. It is significant that the chief American contribution to culture in the past thirty years has been "the higher criticism." England has contributed its Logical Positivism; and although A. J. Ayer has now retreated from his original position to the extent of admitting that Logical Positivism is only a method, not a philosophy, many of his followers still make it an excuse for a complacent, sniping kind of criticism that has no relation to creative thinking. Freudian analysis has now become so important in American life that it might be said to have replaced democracy as the basic American ideology. The result has been a steep decline in all forms of imaginative creation. (It is hard to imagine how Poe or Dostoevsky would have thrived in a society that insisted on explaining their complexes to them.)

The first step of a new existentialism is bound to be the

negative one of attacking Freudianism, Marxism, Logical
Positivism, and any other "ism" that fosters the insignificance fallacy and distracts attention from the need for
creative effort. As a philosophy, existentialism must emphasize the primacy of the will, the importance of the
individual, the final unpredictability and freedom of even
the most neurotic and conditioned human being.

These conclusions may sound disappointingly vague
after the sociological analyses of Part One, but they are
necessarily so. The real work still remains to be done;
these comments are only attempts to foresee its direction.

A Postscript

IN THE TWO years during which the subject of this essay has been forming in my mind, I have given a great many lectures on the hero. It soon became apparent to me that it was going to be less easy to present than I had imagined. My reaction to the unheroic premise in most modern writers was so clear and well-defined that I had supposed that my audiences would find it equally obvious. But the questions they asked soon made it plain that the concept is not as self-evident as I had hoped. A favorite question was: "Where do you hope to find your new hero?" as if I intended putting an advertisement in the *Times* agony column. Another reaction that I invariably met ran something like this: "Don't you think that there are more heroes around today than you realize? The ordinary man in the street . . ." This objection might be followed by an example of someone's next-door neighbor who has had fourteen operations for appendicitis but has never complained. I felt rather in the position of Doña Ana in *Man and Superman:*

> ANA: *Tell me, where can I find the Superman?*
> THE DEVIL: *He is not yet created, Señora.*
> THE STATUE: *And probably never will be. . . .*
> ANA: *Not yet created! Then my work is not yet done.*

But on one occasion, when I said something of the kind, a member of the audience commented that in that case the hero was my business, and perhaps I would do better to try to create him instead of giving lectures to explain why he had disappeared. Although this struck me immediately as justified, I replied that my lecture could help towards the creation of the hero; as far as I was concerned, it served a very definite function: to clarify my ideas. And this still strikes me as the primary justification of a book such as this: to bring these ideas into the daylight of common acceptance. I have corresponded and talked with two of the authors of whom I have written in this book; neither of them seemed to understand what I was getting at. One of them gave an interview to a Paris newspaper in which he spoke of my interest in this subject, and commented: "But since Carlyle we know that nothing is more boring then heroism." The same writer has suggested, in a letter to me, that the hero is a substitute for good government.

These misunderstandings suggest to me that greater precision is required in defining the hero. The queries I have mentioned above were raised at the end of a long lecture on the hero; the writer in question had also discussed the subject with me at some length. Plainly, the image evoked for me by the word "hero" is completely different from that evoked for other people.

TALKING ONLY ABOUT YOURSELF AS A HERO.

There are many possible causes for this. For a generation older than my own, the word arouses memories of Nazi rallies, Mussolini's march on Rome, and so on. Even if its associations are less definite, there is a vague impression of self-glorification, of complacency, of "Mr. Hemingway hiding behind the hair on his chest." And yet these

associations really have very little to do with the word
"heroic." Fundamentally, the heroic urge is only the
desire of life to find a broader field for its powers. Nietzsche
asked: "What is happiness?" and answered: "The feeling
that power is growing, that resistance has been overcome."
Nowadays, the idea of growing power is associated with
sadism, or acts of political aggression. The same dubious
association is attached to the idea of the superman, although a superman would also have a super moral vision
and would consequently be more like the conventional
idea of a saint than of a sadist. This is why the Riesman-
Whyte approach to the problem is inadequate. It may
be invaluable for diagnosing the anti-individualist tendency that is eating away the foundations of modern
society, but it fails to emphasize that the *first* characteristic
of the inner-directed man should be a higher intellectual
and moral perception. If this were not so, there would be
no problem of the hero, and heroes would be two a penny.

This question of moral and intellectual vision has never
been a general problem for society; it has always been
the problem of a limited number of saints, artists, thinkers.
If they abandon it, there is no one to carry it forward; it is
useless to look to popular religious or political movements
for new values. This is one of the most ominous aspects
of the modern world. The writers and thinkers are becoming increasingly other-directed, while the saints are
as rare as ever (and the few men who possess saintly qualities — Schweitzer in Africa, Dolci in Sicily — have a full-
time job relieving human misery, without concerning
themselves with new values). In the literary world particularly, it has come to be accepted that no new Tolstoys
or Shaws can be expected, and the reviewer has put his

yardstick in a cupboard and uses a six-inch ruler for his
weekly batch of novels. And yet a vague, frustrated desire
for the heroic remains, no matter how overlaid by current
standards, and when a play like *Look Back in Anger* or a
novel like Patrick White's *Voss* portrays a man who is a
little more fanatical than the average, the yardsticks are
hastily produced, and the great names begin to fly. (A
book critic of the *Sunday Times* somewhat rashly compared
Voss with *War and Peace*.) Meanwhile, the young writer
displays a weary acceptance of the idea that he can never
produce anything that will rival Joyce or Proust, and con-
centrates on new technical devices to stimulate the interest of *avant-garde* critics.

All this springs from an acceptance of the idea that we
live in an age of decline. But is this true? What evidence
have we that we are tireder, more exhausted, than the
Elizabethans or the Victorians? What is usually regarded
as evidence — the increased crime rate, the teen-age idols,
and so on — is really neither here nor there. We know
that the challenges we face are some of the greatest in
human history, but what evidence have we that we are
less competent to deal with them than the Elizabethans
would have been? It seems likely that we are far more
competent; the ordinary man of today has to deal with
a far greater complexity than his counterpart of four
hundred years ago. The poets who write about despair
and exhaustion deny the reality of modern life: that the
raw, brutal urge for more life struggles as violently as ever
to find expression. The writers who insist that the death-
wish has become a commonplace only prove that they are
completely alienated from the commonplace.

The picture we are faced with, then, is of a society which is neither more nor less decadent than in any previous age, but whose artists and writers have allowed themselves to sink into a minor role. The value of the artist lies in the fact that he asserts a sense of order, of the power of the human spirit, into the sordid conflict of our everyday lives. He sees all life as a battle between chaos and order. It is the vision of order, of conquest of the obstacles and complications of living, that inspires men with new energy and purpose. Life is inconceivable without this vision of purpose. The works of Plato, Mozart, Shaw, represent an ideal that keeps civilization moving forward: the possibility that men of the future might no longer be forced to stumble and fumble through lives of unending trivialities, but might somehow live with the gaiety and power of the Jupiter Symphony, an unbroken drive. The nineteenth century saw this vision reaching a high tide of optimism, with slogans about "culture," "progress," "civilization." Unfortunately, its vision of progress was almost purely intellectual; it preferred to ignore the human realities. When the twentieth century made it obvious that nineteenth-century progress was mostly daydreaming, there was a swing to the opposite extreme, an equally undiscriminating pessimism. E. M. Forster was right when he called *Ulysses* "an attempt to make darkness and dirt succeed where sweetness and light failed." He might have gone further and characterized the whole of modern culture as an attempt to make cynicism and despair succeed where enthusiasm and optimism had failed. With such foundations, it is hardly surprising that the culture of the mid-twentieth century is a monument to the unheroic premise.

But the fact that Victorian optimism was premature is no final argument against optimism. It is only an indication of the need for a more determined realism. Mozart's operas can never become outdated in the same way as Matthew Arnold's *Culture and Anarchy*; their power is deeper than the intellect. The music of Sibelius and Carl Orff will outlast the philosophies of Bertrand Russell and Professor Ayer for the same reason. The necessity of today is a revival of the sense of order; but not a purely intellectual order. When Socrates told Cebes about his recurrent dream in which he was ordered to study music, he was expressing the idea that drives modern existentialism. This order must reach beyond intellect as music does. The art and philosophy of the twentieth century must be rebuilt on foundations in which the words "purpose," "optimism," "idealism" are given a new meaning. And the instrument for creating these new meanings is existential philosophy.

But what can be suggested, by way of concrete solutions? To begin with, it must be accepted that nothing can be done on a popular level. It is the natural impulse of the thinker to hope that his ideas can move great masses of people; the example of Karl Marx lures him like a will-o'-the-wisp. But Marx's thinking has led to the largest other-directed state in the world, for its essence was other-direction. Inner-directed thought (which is to say, existential thought) cannot, by its nature, hope for some mass vehicle for its interpretation. If it is to gain influence, it will do so by infiltration from the higher levels downward. A thinker like Camus has recognized and accepted this.

But the existential thinker has one consolation. He

may never be a Karl Marx, but he has only to look to the examples of Joyce and Eliot to see how wide the influence of the solitary worker can be.

This indicates plainly that any solution offered cannot be popular in the sense that Marxism has become popular. The very nature of Riesman's analysis makes it impossible for him to develop remedies. But this limitation is no cause for pessimism. On the contrary, when the relation of existential thought to the historical situation has been grasped, it might be a cause for optimism. (After all, Buddhism was a form of existentialism in the fifth century B.C.)

In short, if there is to be a revolution, it will have to begin as a cultural revolution. The reason for the defeatism that underlies so much modern writing is the feeling that nothing that happens in the cultural world can have any bearing on the world of practical events. But no major thinker has ever been so modest about the claims of his subject. Plato declared that philosophy is the greatest good that was or ever will be given by the gods to mortal men, and his attitude is typically existentialist; he did not regard thought as an activity of the *avant-garde*. This is the sense that has been lost in the present age, the sense of the immediacy of thought, the way in which thought is meant to be an instrument by which a man learns to dominate his own life.

Stuart Holroyd has written: "In our time, the writer who does not dare to be great cannot hope to be anything." * This penetrates to the heart of the problem. But unfortunately, the meaning attached to the word "great" has begun to incorporate notions of complacency

* "A Writer's Prospect," the *London Magazine*, January, 1959.

and egoism. The lifelong effort of writers such as Flaubert or Yeats is forgotten; instead, one thinks of Shaw's ironic bursts of self-praise, or the posturing of a Mussolini. There is an automatic assumption that belief in oneself is a form of self-delusion. This is the major cultural heresy of the twentieth century, the very foundation of the unheroic premise, the central cause of the cultural slump in our time. Until it is destroyed, there can be no hope for a cultural revival. It is a sign of our age that inner-direction is regarded with suspicion and a certain amount of fear and that any expression of self-belief stands in danger of ridicule. Thought becomes blurred; the inner-directed man expects to be attacked for selfishness.

But the chief necessity of our age is to dare to be inner-directed. This is not easy. Behind us is the rise of fascism, the extermination of millions of Jews, the disappearance of the old order; we live in a world of constant political tension, with a permanent threat of world communism, and a world in which all writers would be expected to be grateful for state supervision. It is no longer a mere figure of rhetoric to say that man's freedom is being destroyed every day. In such a situation, it is hardly surprising that men are losing their sense of interior certainty and becoming more other-directed. Yet it is impossible for man to regain his power over his situation without turning away from the immediacy of his experience and concentrating upon his intuitions of his own value. This turning away is not a form of escapism; it is only the first step in regaining detachment and, eventually, the control that comes with detachment. The solution lies in a deepening of subjectivity, and an analysis of the problems that possesses the confidence of subjectivity. The claptrap about commit-

ment must be rejected without compunction. Commitment cannot be imposed as a duty; its impulse originates in
self-belief. The impulse that for four centuries has expressed itself in scientific discovery must be redirected.
The field of man's subjectivity is still unexplored.

The responsibility of literature in the twentieth century
becomes appallingly clear: to illuminate man's freedom.

POEMS
for You
★ 1 ★

A Four-Book Course for Primary Schools

Compiled by
V. and R. SIBLEY

ILLUSTRATED BY GILBERT DUNLOP

LONDON AND GLASGOW

COLLINS CLEAR-TYPE PRESS

Seventh Impression, 1977

*Printed in Great Britain at the Press of
the Publishers, Cathedral Street, Glasgow*

Contents

3

4

FAIRIES AND FANCY

THINGS TO EAT

PEOPLE

STRANGE PEOPLE AND THINGS

TIME FOR PLAY

MYSELF

THOSE WE LOVE

LIVING THINGS

Hurt no living thing,
Ladybird, nor butterfly,
Nor moth with dusty wing,
Nor cricket chirping cheerily,
Nor grasshopper so light of leap,
Nor dancing gnat, nor beetle fat,
Nor harmless worms that creep.

Christina Rossetti

Birds

LITTLE ROBIN

Come here, little robin, and don't be afraid,
　I would not hurt even a feather;
Come here, little robin, and pick up some bread,
　To feed you this very cold weather.

The winter has come, but it will not stay long,
　And summer we soon shall be greeting;
Then remember, dear robin, to sing me a song
　In return for the breakfast you're eating.

THE LITTLE BIRD

Once I saw a little bird
    Come hop, hop, hop,
And I cried, " Little bird,
    Will you stop, stop, stop ? "

I was going to the window
    To say, " How do you do ? "
But he shook his little tail
    And away he flew.

THE NEST

An ivy wall, a mossy stone,
And someone watching there alone—
A mother with her babies small,
The little keepers of the wall.

Hide safely, little fluffy things,
Fold softly, little mother-wings;
I would not harm a single feather,
So cuddle closer up together!

TOWN SPARROWS

Little town sparrows
So dabbled and dowdy,
Chirping in gutters,
If I had your wings,
I'd fly to the fields where
So spruce and so rowdy,
Your bright little brother,
The country bird sings!

THE BLACKBIRD

In the far corner
close by the swings,
every morning
a blackbird sings.

His bill's so yellow,
his coat's so black,
that he makes a fellow
whistle back.

Ann, my daughter,
thinks that he
sings for us two
especially.

Humbert Wolfe

9

TIME TO RISE

A birdie with a yellow bill
Hopped upon the window sill,
Cocked his shining eye and said;
" Ain't you 'shamed, you sleepy-head ? "

Robert Louis Stevenson

MRS. PECK PIGEON

Mrs. Peck Pigeon
   Is picking for bread;
Bob, bob, bob,
   Goes her little round head.

Tame as a pussy cat
   In the street,
Step, step, step,
   Go her little red feet.

With her little red feet
   And her little round head
Mrs. Peck Pigeon
   Goes picking for bread.

Eleanor Farjeon

DICKY-BIRDS

Two little dicky-birds
    Sitting on a twig,
Both very plump
    And neither very big.

" Tweet ? " said the first one,
    " Cheep ! " said his brother—
Wasn't that a funny way
    To talk to one another ?

Down flew one bird
    And picked up a crust;
Off went the other
    To a little heap of dust;

Plunged into a dust bath,
    All puffed out and fat,
Wouldn't it be very strange
    To have a bath like that ?

Both little brown birds
    At the set of sun
Flew into a big tree
    Because the day was done.

Cuddled in a warm nest,
    Cosy as could be,
Mustn't it be lovely
    Sleeping in a tree ?

Natalie Joan

THE VULTURE

The vulture eats between his meals,
    And that's the reason why
He very, very rarely feels
    As well as you or I.

His eye is dull, his head is bald,
    His neck is growing thinner.
Oh ! what a lesson for us all
    To only eat at dinner !

Hilaire Belloc

Animals

TO A SQUIRREL AT KYLE-NA-NO

Come play with me;
Why should you run
Through the shaking tree
As though I'd a gun
To strike you dead ?
When all I would do
Is to scratch your head
And let you go.

W. B. Yeats

12

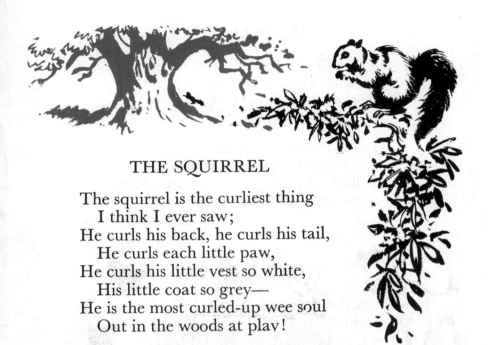

THE SQUIRREL

The squirrel is the curliest thing
  I think I ever saw;
He curls his back, he curls his tail,
  He curls each little paw,
He curls his little vest so white,
  His little coat so grey—
He is the most curled-up wee soul
  Out in the woods at play!

LOOKING AHEAD

Bushy-tailed squirrels are busy as bees,
Hiding their nuts in the cupboards of trees,
Raiding the oak trees, and storing away
Acorn provisions for some winter's day.

For mornings are misty and evenings grow cold,
And late-clinging leaves on the trees are all gold,
So squirrels prepare as they tumble and leap
Their mid-winter breakfast, then curl up to sleep.

Annie Wrench

THE RABBITS

The little furry rabbits,
    Keep very, very still,
And peep at me across the grass
    As I walk up the hill.

But if I venture nearer
    To join them at their play,
A flash of white, and they are gone,
    Not one of them will stay.

Lucy Diamond

THE DORMOUSE

Hush! for the dormouse is dreaming
    Of sunshine, and poppies, and wheat;
Though frost fairies dance round his cradle,
    He hears not the tap of their feet.

Soundly the dormouse is sleeping!
    His tail is curled round him in bed;
He has nice withered leaves for his bed-clothes,
    A pillow of moss for his head.

When Spring through the woodlands comes singing,
    He hears her light step in the lane;
And sighs, as he lazily stretches—
    " Dear me! Is it morning again ? "

Charlotte Druitt Cole

TWO NAMES

" Bow-wow, little dog, have you any name ? "
" Yes, sir, two, but they don't mean the same;
One from my master, he calls me Champ,
And one from the neighbours, they call me SCAMP! "

TIM

I've got a dog and his name is Tim.
I think an awful lot of him.
His coat is shaggy
And a little bit raggy—
But his tail is waggy
And his bright eyes shine.
One ear sticks up and the other flops down,
I bought him as a pup for half-a-crown,
We run in the park,
We frolic and we lark,
He's got a loud bark
And he's mine, all mine.

Diane Leslie

MY DOG

Have you seen a little dog anywhere about ?
A raggy dog, a shaggy dog, who's always looking out
For some fresh mischief which he thinks he really ought
    to do.
He's very likely, at this minute, biting someone's shoe.

If you see that little dog, his tail up in the air,
A whirly tail, a curly tail, a dog who doesn't care
For any other dog he meets, not even for himself,
Then hide your mats, and put your meat upon the top-
    most shelf.

If you see a little dog, barking at the cars,
A raggy dog, a shaggy dog, with eyes like twinkling stars,
Just let me know, for though he's bad, as bad as bad can
    be,
I wouldn't change that dog for all the treasures of the
    sea!

Emily Lewis

THE TABBY CAT

If you have a tabby cat,
    If you want to please him,
Tie a ribbon round his neck,
    Never, never tease him.
Tabby cats are grave and stately,
And they like to act sedately.

Agnes G. Herbertson

KILKENNY CATS

There were once two cats of Kilkenny,
Each thought there was one cat too many;

So they fought and they fit,
And they scratched and they bit,

Till, excepting their nails
And the tips of their tails,
Instead of two cats there weren't any.

MARY AND HER KITTEN

The kitten's in the dairy!
Where's our Mary?
She isn't in the kitchen,
She isn't at her stitching,
She isn't at the weeding,
The brewing, or the kneading!

Mary's in the garden, walking in a dream,
Mary's got her fancies, and *the kitten's got the cream!*

Eleanor Farjeon

KITTY AND MOUSIE

Once there was a little kitty
   White as the snow;
In a barn she used to frolic
   Long time ago.

In the barn a little mousie
   Ran to and fro,
For she heard the little kitty
   Long time ago.

Two black eyes had little kitty,
   Black as a sloe;
And they spied the little mousie
   Long time ago.

Four soft paws had little kitty,
   Paws soft as snow;
And they caught the little mousie
   Long time ago.

Nine pearl teeth had little kitty,
   All in a row,
And they bit the little mousie
   Long time ago.

When the teeth bit little mousie,
   Mousie cried out, " Oh! "
But she slipped away from kitty
   Long time ago.

           E. Prentiss

MICE

I think mice
Are rather nice.

Their tails are long,
Their faces small,
They haven't any
Chins at all.
Their ears are pink,
Their teeth are white,
They run about
The house at night.
They nibble things
They shouldn't touch
And no one seems
To like them much.

But I think mice
Are nice.

Rose Fyleman

THE TWO RATS

He was a rat, and she was a rat,
   And down in one hole they did dwell;
And both were as black as a witch's cat,
   And they loved each other well.

He had a tail, and she had a tail,
   Both long, and curling, and fine;
And each said, " Yours is the finest tail
   In the world, excepting mine."

He smelt the cheese, and she smelt the cheese,
   And they both pronounced it good;
And both remarked it would greatly add
   To the charms of their daily food.

So he ventured out, and she ventured out,
   And I saw them go with pain;
For what befell them I never can tell,
   For they never came back again.

MY GOLDFISH

All day long he swims around
  His little home of glass;
He never smiles, he never frowns:
  I watch him pass and pass.

Round the globe and round again;
  Makes me dizzy watching;
Open mouth, then shut again;
  Wonder what he's catching?

Shining like a piece of gold
  Glistening like a star;
Never winking, never blinking—
  Round and round the jar.

Round the globe and round again;
  Tail and fins a-quivering,
Living in the water cold:
  Wonder if he's shivering?

He's a faithful little friend,
  I always know I'll find him
Swimming gravely round and round
  With his tail behind him.

Round the globe and round again,
  Round eyes never blinking;
Looking very, very wise:
  Wonder what he's thinking?

John R. Crossland

A FRIEND IN THE GARDEN

He is not John, the gardener,
    And yet the whole day long
Employs himself most usefully,
    The flower-beds among.

He is not Tom, the pussy-cat,
    And yet the other day,
With stealthy stride and glistening eye,
    He crept upon his prey.

He is not Dash, the dear old dog,
    And yet, perhaps, if you
Took pains with him and petted him,
    You'd come to love him too.

He's not a blackbird, though he chirps,
    And though he once was black;
And now he wears a loose grey coat,
    All wrinkled on the back.

He's got a very dirty face,
    And very shining eyes!
He sometimes comes and sits indoors;
    He looks—and p'r'aps is—wise.

But in a sunny flower-bed
    He has his fixed abode;
He eats the things that eat my plants—
    He is a friendly TOAD.

Juliana Horatia Ewing

DUCKS

Mother likes her black hen
  That lays an egg and clucks.
Father likes his new car,
  But I like ducks.

I like their fronts.
  I like their backs.
I like their waddle.
  I like their " Quacks ".

Bobby likes his toy train
  With its yellow trucks.
Betty likes her baby doll.

  But I like ducks.
                Mary Daunt

TWO DUCKS

Two ducks went waddling down the lane;
Said one to the other, " What beautiful rain! "
Two children came to the door with a frown,
They couldn't run out while the rain poured down.
The Clerk of the Weather scratched his head;
" You can't please everyone," he said.

23

SPIDERS AND FLIES

While flies can travel
Here and there,
And spiders can't
Go anywhere,
I wish I knew
The reason why
The spider always
Gets the fly.

Elizabeth Fleming

THE FLY

How large unto the tiny fly
Must little things appear!—
A rosebud like a feather bed,
Its prickle like a spear;

A dewdrop like a looking-glass,
A hair like golden wire;
The smallest grain of mustard-seed
As fierce as coals of fire;

A loaf of bread, a lofty hill;
A wasp, a cruel leopard;
And specks of salt as bright to see
As lambkins to a shepherd.

Walter de la Mare

24

MY PONY

I had a little pony,
   His name was Dapple-grey,
I lent him to a lady,
   To ride a mile away;
She whipped him, she slashed him,
   She rode him through the mire;
I would not lend my pony now
   For all the lady's hire.

GRASSHOPPER GREEN

Grasshopper Green is a comical chap;
   He lives on the best of fare.
Bright little trousers, jacket and cap,
   These are his summer wear.
Out in the meadow he loves to go,
   Playing away in the sun;
It's hopperty, skipperty, high and low,
   Summer's the time for fun.

Grasshopper Green has a quaint little house;
   It's under the hedge so gay.
Grandmother Spider, as still as a mouse,
   Watches him over the way.
Gladly he's calling the children, I know,
   Out in the beautiful sun;
It's hopperty, skipperty, high and low,
   Summer's the time for fun.

CIRCUS

Giraffes are tall,
  And their heads are high.
They stare at people
  As they go by.

Tigers are long,
  And painted with dyes.
They have soft whiskers
  And yellow eyes.

Camels hump up
  Where they should hump down.
Their tails are limp
  And furry and brown.

They can't do tricks,
  Like the bears and the seals,
But they're all of them very
  Prompt to meals.

                Marchette Chute

26

IF I MET . . .

If I met a crow—
  I should say, " *Caa-Caa !* "
If I met a lamb—
  I should say, " *Baa-Baa !* "
If I met a cow—
  I should say, " *Moo-Moo !* "
If I met a dove—
  I should say, " *Boo-Coo !* "
If I met a dog—
  I should say, " *Bow-Wow !* "
If I met a cat—
  I should say, " *Mi-aouw !* "
If I met a crocodile—
  What should I say ?
Why—nothing at all !
  I *should*—
      just—
        RUN AWAY !

Queenie Scott-Hopper

On the Farm

THE HEN

A white hen sitting
    On white eggs three;
Next, three speckled chickens
    As plump as plump can be.

An owl and a hawk
    And a bat come to see;
But chicks beneath their mother's wing
    Squat safe as safe can be.

Christina Rossetti

THE CLUCKING HEN

" Will you take a walk with me,
    My little wife, today ?
There's barley in the barley-field,
    And hay-seed in the hay."

" Thank you," said the clucking hen;
    " I've something else to do;
I'm busy sitting on my eggs,
    I cannot walk with you."

" Cluck, cluck, cluck, cluck,"
  Said the clucking hen;
" My little chicks will soon be hatched,
  I'll think about it then."

The clucking hen sat on her nest,
  She made it in the hay;
And warm and snug beneath her breast
  A dozen white eggs lay.

Crack, crack, went all the eggs,
  Out popped the chickens small!
" Cluck," said the clucking hen,
  " Now I have you all."

" Come along, my little chicks,
  I'll take a walk with *you*."
" Hello! " said the barn-door cock,
  " Cock-a-doodle-doo! "

THE CHICKENS

Said the first little chicken
  With a queer little squirm,
" I wish I could find
  A fat little worm."

Said the next little chicken
  With an odd little shrug,
" I wish I could find
  A fat little slug."

Said the third little chicken
  With a sharp little squeal,
" I wish I could find
  Some nice yellow meal."

Said the fourth little chicken
  With a small sigh of grief,
" I wish I could find
  A little green leaf."

Said the fifth little chicken
  With a faint little moan,
" I wish I could find
  A wee gravel stone."

" Now, see here," said the mother,
  From the green garden patch,
" If you want any breakfast,
  Just come here and scratch."

PAUL THE PIG

Paul the pig
Cared not a fig
For small nor big,
   Not he;
For man, nor child,
Nor woman mild,
Nor urchin wild,
   Not he.

He'd push his snout
And grub and rout
All round about,
   Would he:
With nose so blunt
He'd snort and grunt,
For something hunt,
   Would he.

He'd blink his eyes,
He was so wise,
For all his size,
   Was he:
He cared no jot
For aught but what
To eat he got,
   Did he.

LITTLE LAMBS

When it is cold
On down and wold
And a fleece of snow
Falls over the fold,
The small new lambs
Creep close to the fleece
Of the big old dams
And sleep in peace.

When it is green
On hill and dene
And the frisky sun
On the fold is seen,
The small new lambs
From the shelter run
Of the big old dams
To frisk in the sun.

Eleanor Farjeon

THE HAPPY SHEEP

All through the night the happy sheep
Lie in the meadow grass asleep.

Their wool keeps out the frost and rain
Until the sun comes round again.

They have no buttons to undo,
Nor hair to brush like me and you.

And with the light they lift their heads
To find their breakfast on their beds,

Or rise and walk about and eat
The carpet underneath their feet.

Wilfrid Thorley

The World of Nature

AUTUMN

Yellow the bracken,
  Golden the sheaves,
Rosy the apples,
  Crimson the leaves;
Mist on the hillside,
  Clouds grey and white,
Autumn, good morning,
  Summer, good night!

Florence Hoatson

33

APPLE HARVEST

O down in the orchard
  ' Tis harvesting time,
And up the tall ladders
  The fruit pickers climb.

Among the green branches
  That sway overhead
The apples are hanging
  All rosy and red.

Just ripe for the picking,
  All juicy and sweet!
So pretty to look at
  And lovely to eat!

Helen Leuty

34

THE LEAVES

" Come, little leaves," said the wind one day,
" Come o'er the meadows with me and play;
Put on your dresses of red and gold,
For summer is gone and the days grow cold."

Soon as the leaves heard the wind's loud call,
Down they came fluttering, one and all;
Over the brown fields they danced and flew,
Singing the sweet little song they knew.

Dancing and whirling, the little leaves went,
Winter had called them, and they were content;
Soon, fast asleep in their earthy beds,
The snow laid a coverlet over their heads.

George Cooper

JACK FROST

Look out! Look out!
Jack Frost is about!
   He's after our fingers and toes;
And, all through the night,
The gay little sprite,
   Is working when nobody knows.

He'll climb each tree,
So nimble is he;
   His silvery powder he'll shake;
To windows he'll creep,
And while we're asleep,
   Such wonderful pictures he'll make.

Cecily E. Pike

35

WHITE FIELDS

In the winter time we go
Walking in the fields of snow;
Where there is no grass at all;
Where the top of every wall,
Every fence, and every tree,
Is as white as white can be.

Pointing out the way we came,
—Every one of them the same—
All across the fields there be
Prints in silver filigree;
And our mothers always know,
By the footprints in the snow,
Where it is the children go.

James Stephens

MY LADY SPRING

My Lady Spring is dressed in green,
    She wears a primrose crown,
And little baby buds and twigs
    Are clinging to her gown;
The sun shines if she laughs at all,
But if she weeps the raindrops fall.

SPRING

Spring is coming, spring is coming;
  Birdies, build your nest;
Weave together straw and feather,
  Doing each your best.

Spring is coming, spring is coming;
  Flowers are coming too;
Pansies, lilies, daffodillies
  Now are coming through.

Spring is coming, spring is coming;
  All around is fair;
Shimmer and quiver on the river,
  Joy is everywhere.

William Blake

IN THE MEADOW

A frisky lamb
And a frisky child
Playing their pranks
In a cowslip meadow:
The sky all blue
And the air all mild
And the fields all sun
And the lanes half shadow.

Christina Rossetti

37

SNOWDROP TIME

" 'Tis rather dark in the earth today,"
Said one little bulb to his brother;
" But I thought that I felt a sunbeam ray—
We must strive and grow till we find the way! "
And they nestled close to each other.
Then they struggled and toiled by day and by night,
Till two little snowdrops in green and white
Rose out of the darkness and into the light,
And softly kissed one another.

Annie Matheson

THE SNOWDROPS

" Where are the snowdrops ? " said the sun.
" Dead! " said the frost,
" Buried and lost—
Every one! "

" A foolish answer," said the sun;
" They did not die.
Asleep they lie—
Every one!

" And I will wake them, I, the sun,
Into the light,
All clad in white—
Every one! "

Annie Matheson

DAFFODOWNDILLY

She wore her yellow sun-bonnet,
  She wore her greenest gown;
She turned to the south wind
  And curtsied up and down.
She turned to the sunlight
  And shook her yellow head,
And whispered to her neighbour:
  " Winter is dead."

A. A. Milne

THE LITTLE PLANT

In the heart of a seed,
  Buried deep, so deep,
A dear little plant
  Lay fast asleep.

" Wake," said the sunshine,
  " And creep to the light."
" Wake," said the voice
  Of the raindrops bright.

The little plant heard,
  And it rose to see
What the wonderful outside
  World might be.

Kate L. Brown

THE FIELD DAISY

I'm a pretty little thing,
Always coming with the spring;
In the meadows green I'm found,
Peeping just above the ground,
And my stalk is covered flat,
With a white and yellow hat.

Little children, when you pass
Lightly o'er the tender grass,
Skip about, but do not tread
On my bright but lowly head,
For I always seem to say,
" Surly winter's gone away. "

Jane Taylor

TREES

The Oak is called the King of Trees,
The Aspen quivers in the breeze,
The Poplar grows up straight and tall,
The Pear tree spreads along the wall,
The Sycamore gives pleasant shade,
The Willow droops in watery glade,
The Fir tree useful timber gives,
The Beech amid the forest lives.

Sara Coleridge

THE BEECH TREE

I'd like to have a garden
 With a beech tree on the lawn;
The little birds that lived there
 Would wake me up at dawn.

And in the summer weather
 When all the leaves were green,
I'd sit beneath the beech-boughs
 And see the sky between.

Rose Fyleman

BED IN SUMMER

In winter I get up at night
And dress by yellow candle-light.
In summer, quite the other way,
I have to go to bed by day.

I have to go to bed and see
The birds still hopping on the tree,
Or hear the grown-up people's feet
Still going past me in the street.

And does it not seem hard to you,
When all the sky is clear and blue,
And I should like so much to play,
To have to go to bed by day ?

Robert Louis Stevenson

WATER JEWELS

A million little diamonds twinkled on the trees;
And all the little maidens said, " A jewel, if you please ! "
But when they held their hands out-stretched to catch the
    diamonds gay,
A million little sunbeams came and stole them all away.

Mary Butts

DAISIES

At evening when I go to bed,
I see the stars shine overhead;
They are the little daisies white
That dot the meadow of the night.

And often while I'm dreaming so,
Across the sky the moon will go;
It is a lady, sweet and fair,
Who comes to gather daisies there.

For, when at morning I arise,
There's not a star left in the skies;
She's picked them all and dropped them down
Into the meadows of the town.

Frank Dempster Sherman

THE MOON

Oh, look at the Moon;
   She is shining up there.
Oh, Mother, she looks
   Like a lamp in the air!

Last week she was smaller,
   And shaped like a bow,
But now she's grown bigger,
   And round as an O.

Pretty Moon, pretty Moon,
   How you shine on the door,
And make it all bright
   On my nursery floor!

You shine on my playthings,
   And show me their place,
And I love to look up
   At your pretty bright face.

And there is the star
   Close by you, and maybe
That small, twinkling star
   Is your little baby.

Eliza Lee Follen

THE MOON

The moon has a face like the clock in the hall;
She shines on thieves on the garden wall,
On streets and fields and harbour quays,
And birdies asleep in the forks of the trees.

The squalling cat and the squeaking mouse,
The howling dog by the door of the house,
The bat that lies in bed at noon,
All love to be out by the light of the moon.

But all of the things that belong to the day
Cuddle to sleep to be out of her way;
And flowers and children close their eyes
Till up in the morning the sun shall rise.

Robert Louis Stevenson

SOMEBODY'S ALWAYS PLEASED

Who likes the rain ?
" I," said the duck,
" I think I'm in luck
When I've plenty of puddles to splash in again! "

Who likes the breeze ?
"I," said the oak,
" It's such a joke
To throw off my old leaves as fast as I please! "

Who likes the sun ?
" I," said the spider,
" I make my web wider,
For flies love the sunshine—I'll catch every one! "

Who likes the snow ?
" I," said the boy,
" I think it's a joy
To have such a lot of fine snowballs to throw! "

Enid Blyton

SOMETIMES

Sometimes wind, and sometimes rain,
Then the sun comes back again;
Sometimes rain and sometimes snow,
Goodness, how we'd like to know
Why the weather alters so.

Ford Madox Ford

BOATS SAIL ON THE RIVERS

Boats sail on the rivers,
  And ships sail on the seas;
But clouds that sail across the sky
  Are prettier far than these.

There are bridges on the rivers,
  As pretty as you please;
But the bow that bridges heaven,
  And overtops the trees,
And builds a road from earth to sky,
  Is prettier far than these.

Christina Rossetti

THE WIND

Who has seen the wind ?
  Neither I nor you:
But when the leaves hang trembling,
  The wind is passing through.

Who has seen the wind ?
  Neither you nor I:
But when the trees bow down their heads,
  The wind is passing by.

O Wind, why do you never rest,
  Wandering, whistling to and fro,
Bringing rain out of the west,
  From the dim north bringing snow ?

Christina Rossetti

NIGHT

The sun that shines all day so bright,
I wonder where he goes at night.
He sinks behind a distant hill
And all the world grows dark and still,
And then I go to bed and sleep
Until the day begins to peep.
And when my eyes unclose, I see
The sun is shining down on me.

While we are fast asleep in bed
The sun must go, I've heard it said,
To other countries far away,
To make them warm and bright and gay.
If that is so, I hope the sun,
When all his nightly work is done,
Will not forget to come again
And wake me through the window-pane.

A FAIRY RING

If you see a fairy ring
    In a field of grass,
Very lightly step around,
    Tiptoe as you pass;
Last night fairies frolicked there,
And they're sleeping somewhere near.

If you see a tiny fay
    Lying fast asleep,
Shut your eyes and run away,
    Do not stay to peep;
And be sure you *never* tell,
Or you'll break a fairy spell.

THE LITTLE ELF-MAN

I met a little elf-man once
    Down where the lilies blow.
I asked him why he was so small,
    And why he didn't grow.

He slightly frowned, and with his eye
    He looked me through and through—
" I'm just as big for me," said he,
    " As you are big for you! "

J. K. Bangs

THE WITCH

I saw her plucking cowslips,
    And marked her where she stood,
She never knew I watched her
    While hiding in the wood.

Her skirt was brightest crimson,
    And black her steeple hat,
Her broomstick lay beside her—
    I'm positive of that.

Her chin was sharp and pointed,
    Her eyes were—I don't know—
For, when she turned towards me—
    I thought it best—to go!

Percy H. Ilott

THE ELF AND THE DORMOUSE

Under a toadstool
   Crept a wee elf
Out of the rain
   To shelter himself.

Under the toadstool
   Sound asleep,
Sat a big dormouse
   All in a heap.

Trembled the wee elf,
   Frightened, and yet
Fearing to fly away,
   Lest he got wet,

To the next shelter
   Maybe a mile!
Sudden the wee elf
   Smiled a wee smile,

Tugged till the toadstool
   Toppled in two,
Holding it over him,
   Gaily he flew.

Soon he was safe home,
   Dry as could be.
Soon woke the dormouse—
   " Good gracious me!

" Where is my toadstool ? "
   Loud he lamented—
And that's how umbrellas
   First were invented.

Oliver Herford

IN SHELTER

What do little fairies do—
I wonder very much, don't you ?—
When it rains, or when it snows,
Or when the bitter north wind blows.

Beneath a mushroom, wide outspread
Like an umbrella overhead,
There together, close they creep,
And at the falling drops they peep.

They do not like the grass to get
All muddy, and the flowers all wet—
They sadly sigh, and sneeze and cough,
" I do so wish it would leave off! "

PLAIN JANE

" Pudding and pie,"
Said Jane—" Oh my! "

" Which would you rather ? "
Asked her father.

" Both! " said Jane,
Quite bold and plain.

PIES

I watched our cook this morning
   Make lovely little pies;
I saw just how she mixed them,
   And then, for a surprise,

I went into the garden,
   And made some out of dirt;
But now I wish I hadn't,
   'Cos Mummy's hands do hurt!

Louisa Pratt

THE CUPBOARD

I know a little cupboard,
With a teeny tiny key,
And there's a jar of lollipops
   For me, me, me.

It has a little shelf, my dear,
As dark as dark can be,
And there's a dish of Banbury cakes
   For me, me, me.

I have a small fat grandmama,
With a very slippery knee,
And she's keeper of the cupboard,
   With a key, key, key.

And when I'm very good, my dear,
As good as good can be,
There's Banbury cakes and lollipops
   For me, me, me.

Walter de la Mare

APPLES

If I were an apple and grew on a tree,
I think I'd drop down on a nice boy like me;
I wouldn't stay there, giving nobody joy;
I'd fall down at once and say, " Eat me, my boy! "

THE PANCAKE

Mix a pancake,
Stir a pancake,
  Pop it in the pan.
Fry the pancake,
Toss the pancake,
  Catch it if you can.

Christina Rossetti

PANCAKES

Someone's making pancakes,
  The girdle's on the grate;
The bowl of batter's beaten up,
  So I am going to wait
Until the work is over,
  And there, perhaps, will be,
Among the brown and speckled ones,
  A yellow one for me!

Elizabeth Fleming

UNCLE

Uncle is the sort of man
   Who comes at an unusual time,
And calls out, " Hullo, kiddies! Can
   You take me to the pantomime ? "

The play's no sooner over than
   He bellows very heartily,
" Well, what about it, kiddies ? Can
   You manage ices for your tea ? "

And without any previous plan,
   When taking leave, as like as not,
He chinks his pockets, shouting, " Can
   You spend five shillings, kiddies, what ? "

Uncle is that sort of man,
And as for us, of course we can!

Eleanor Farjeon

A SAD LITTLE BOY

He put one foot
Before the other,
Then put the other
Before the one,
And that is how
He came to his mother
To say he was sorry
For what he had done.

TWO MERRY MEN

Two merry men
    One summer day
Forsook their toys,
    Forgot their play.

Two little faces
    Full of fun;
Two little hearts
    That beat as one;

Four little hands
    At work with a will;
Four little legs
    That can't keep still;

For labour is sweet,
    And toil is fun,
When mother wants
    Any work done.

WHICH?

The boy speaks:

" Let me hold your horse, Sir,
   I am three years old,
And I am strong and able
   Any horse to hold.

" Mother's in the orchard,
   Father's in the shed,
And your horse looks quiet,
   Let me hold his head."

The horse speaks:

" Let me hold the boy, Sir,
   He is very small,
And I will not kick him,
   Will not bite at all.

" It will give me something,
   Though not much, to do,
Let me hold the boy, Sir,
   While I wait for you."

Edith Nesbit

57

THE PEPPER BOX

Baby found a little box,
    True, it wasn't lost,
Baby, later, found that out,
    Much to Baby's cost:
Full of little holes the top,
    Baby shook it well;
What it was that sprinkled out,
    Perhaps I needn't tell.
Baby's far too young to talk,
    All the same it's true,
Plain as plain, a hundred times,
    Baby said, " At-choo! "

RICE PUDDING

What is the matter with Mary Jane?
She's crying with all her might and main,
And she won't eat her dinner—rice pudding again—
What *is* the matter with Mary Jane?

What is the matter with Mary Jane?
I've promised her dolls and a daisy chain,
And a book about animals—all in vain—
What *is* the matter with Mary Jane?

What is the matter with Mary Jane?
She's perfectly well, and she hasn't a pain;
But look at her, now she's beginning again!
What *is* the matter with Mary Jane?

What is the matter with Mary Jane?
I've promised her sweets and a ride in the train,
And I've begged her to stop for a bit and explain—
What *is* the matter with Mary Jane?

What is the matter with Mary Jane?
She's perfectly well and she hasn't a pain,
And it's lovely rice pudding for dinner again !—
What *is* the matter with Mary Jane?

A. A. Milne

THE LOST BUTTON

Mary Arabella Sue
Lost a button off her shoe!
Searched the whole house, up and down,
Searched the pockets of her gown,
Searched beneath her plate of mutton!
(*What* a place to seek a button!)
Set the whole town in a flurry,
Till they said, " O *bless* that worry,
Mary Arabella Sue,
Searching *all* the houses through!
Can't she buy *another* button?
Plenty in the shops at Sutton!"
So they said, but still she worried,
Once more through the house she hurried,
Found the button *in* her shoe—
Foolish Arabella Sue.

SCARLET ANN

Three jolly gipsies
  Bought a caravan;
They painted it in crimson
  And they called it " Scarlet Ann "!

A hundred miles or so
  " Scarlet Ann " could go
If you coaxed old " Nodding Neddy ",
  And you didn't say, " Whoa."

The wind blew through
  The cracks in " Scarlet Ann ",
So the three jolly gipsies
  Bought a warming-pan.

The warming-pan was brass,
  And it did keep them warm,
But it couldn't keep them dry
  In the big rain-storm.

So the three jolly gipsies
  Left poor " Scarlet Ann ",
And they harnessed " Nodding Neddy "
  To another caravan.

Eileen Mathias

BETTY AT THE PARTY

" When I was at the party,"
    Said Betty, aged just four,
" A little girl fell off her chair
    Right down upon the floor;
And all the other little girls
    Began to laugh, but me—
I didn't laugh a single bit,"
    Said Betty seriously.

" Why not ? " her mother asked her,
    Full of delight to find
That Betty—bless her little heart!—
    Had been so sweetly kind.
" Why didn't you laugh, my darling ?
    Or don't you like to tell ? "
" I didn't laugh," said Betty,
    " 'Cause it was I that fell."

THE EMPTY CHAIR

" Why, what's this chair for, Darling ? "
    To Betty, Mummy said,
When she came to kiss her girlie,
    And tuck her up in bed.
" Oh! that's for my dear Angel,
    Who guards me through the night;
He'd get so tired of standing,
    And I like to be polite! "

Louisa Pratt

JONATHAN GEE

Jonathan Gee
  Went out with his cow;
He climbed up a tree
  And sat on a bough.
He sat on a bough
  And it broke in half,
And John's old cow
  Did nothing but laugh.

Rose Fyleman
(translated from the Dutch)

JACK JINGLE

Jack Jingle went 'prentice
  To make a horse-shoe,
He wasted the iron
  Till it would not do.

His master came in,
  And started to rail;
Says Jack, " The shoe's spoiled,
  But 'twill still make a nail."

He tried at the nail
  But chancing to miss,
" If it won't make a nail,
  It shall yet make a hiss."

Then into the water
  Threw the hot iron, smack!
" Hiss! " quoth the iron;
  " I thought so," said Jack.

THE SAILOR

Across wide seas the sailor goes
To burning lands, to lands of snows;
To bring us meat and wool and wheat,
And other things to wear and eat.

Strange People and Things

SOME ONE

Some one came knocking
    At my wee, small door;
Some one came knocking,
    I'm sure—sure—sure.
I listened, I opened,
    I looked to left and right,
But nought there was a-stirring
    In the still dark night;
Only the busy beetle
    Tap-tapping in the wall,
Only from the forest
    The screech owl's call,
Only the cricket whistling
    While the dewdrops fall,
So I know not who came knocking,
    At all, at all, at all.

Walter de la Mare

63

MISTRESS PEGGY

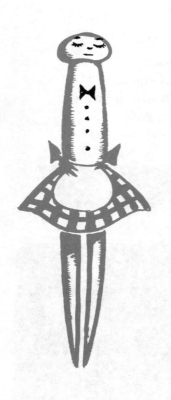

Funny little face,
  Never wears a smile;
Two wooden legs,
  Couldn't walk a mile.

Stupid little head
  Only made of wood;
Yet does her duty
  As everybody should.

Sets her tiny teeth,
  And won't let go,
Never mind how fiercely
  The wind may blow.

She's a very useful
  Good old friend of mine;
Little Mistress Peggy,
  Of the laundry line.

Charlotte Druitt Cole

MR. NOBODY

I know a funny little man,
  As quiet as a mouse,
Who does the mischief that is done,
  In everybody's house!
There's no one ever sees his face,
  And yet we all agree
That every plate we break was cracked
  By Mr. Nobody.

'Tis he who always tears our books,
    Who leaves the door ajar,
He pulls the buttons from our shirts,
    And scatters pins afar;
That squeaking door will always squeak
    For, prithee, don't you see,
We leave the oiling to be done
    By Mr. Nobody.

He puts damp wood upon the fire,
    That kettles cannot boil;
His are the feet that bring in mud,
    And all the carpets soil.
The papers always are mislaid,
    Who had them last but he ?
There's no one tosses them about
    But Mr. Nobody.

The finger marks upon the door
    By none of us are made;
We never leave the blinds unclosed,
    To let the curtains fade.
The ink we never spill, the boots
    That lying round you see
Are not our boots; they all belong
    To Mr. Nobody.

SAMMY SOAPSUDS

When little Sammy Soapsuds
   Went out to take a ride,
In looking over London Bridge
   He fell into the tide.

His parents never having taught
   Their loving Sam to swim,
The tide soon got the mastery,
   And made an end of him.

THE BLOT

I saw a wee man,
   And what do you think ?
His body and clothes
   Were all made of ink!

I felt very sad
   When I saw him fall;
I didn't want him
   To come at all.

But down he came
   Whether welcome or not.
Shall I tell you his name ?
     It was
BIG BLACK BLOT!

M. K. Westcott

MR. SNOWMAN

We made a man all by ourselves;
    We made him jolly fat;
We stuck a pipe into his face,
    And on his head a hat.

We made him stand upon one leg,
    That so he might not walk,
We made his mouth without a tongue,
    That so he might not talk.

We left him grinning on the lawn
    That we to bed might go;
But in the night he ran away,
    Leaving a heap of snow.

Hamish Hendry

THE COLD OLD HOUSE

I know a house, and a cold old house,
    A cold old house by the sea.
If I were a mouse in that cold old house
    What a cold cold mouse I'd be!

PLEASE

There's a magic little word
That works wonders when it's heard,
Though it sometimes seems to lose itself with ease,
But there's such a charm about it,
That we cannot do without it,
And that magic little word is only " Please ".

SEAS

There's a White Sea on the map,
There's a Red and Black Sea, too;
   But the sea I've seen
   Is sometimes green
And sometimes it is blue.

THE SWING

How do you like to go up in a swing,
    Up in the air so blue ?
Oh, I do think it the pleasantest thing
    Ever a child can do!

Up in the air and over the wall,
    Till I can see so wide,
Rivers and trees and cattle and all
    Over the countryside—

Till I look down on the garden green,
    Down on the roof so brown—
Up in the air I go flying again,
    Up in the air and down!

Robert Louis Stevenson

69

FOREIGN LANDS

Up into the cherry tree
Who should climb but little me?
I held the trunk with both my hands,
And looked abroad on foreign lands.

I saw the next-door garden lie,
Adorned with flowers, before my eye,
And many pleasant places more
That I had never seen before.

I saw the dimpling river pass
And be the sky's blue looking-glass;
The dusty roads go up and down
With people tramping in to town.

If I could find a higher tree
Farther and farther I should see,
To where the grown-up river slips
Into the sea among the ships,

To where the roads on either hand
Lead onward into fairyland,
Where all the children dine at five,
And all the playthings come alive.

Robert Louis Stevenson

WHERE GO THE BOATS?

Dark brown is the river,
   Golden is the sand.
It flows along for ever,
   With trees on either hand.

Green leaves a-floating,
   Castles of the foam,
Boats of mine a-boating—
   Where will all come home?

On goes the river,
   And out past the mill,
Away down the valley,
   Away down the hill.

Away down the river,
   A hundred miles or more,
Other little children
   Shall bring my boats ashore.

Robert Louis Stevenson

71

THE DOCTOR

Said Mary, " My dolly
   Is sick, sick, sick;
So run for the doctor,
   Quick, quick, quick."

He came with his cane,
   And he came with his hat;
He came to the door
   With a rat-tat-tat.

He looked at the dolly,
   And then shook his head;
He said, " You must put her
   To bed, bed, bed.

" You must keep her very warm,
   And very, very, still;
And, when I come tomorrow,
   You must pay me my bill."

PADDLING

When I went paddling in the sea,
The sun looked down, and he winked at me,
With a merry smile, as if to say:
" Yes, it's a perfect paddling day! "

The breeze blew playfully round my head;
It tickled my ear, and softly said:
" Paddle away, child, don't you miss
One bit of the sea on a day like this! "

The waves went rippling, quiet and slow,
But I heard them say, as I bent down low:
" Now, little boy, don't go too far,
You'll get *quite* wet enough where you are! "

Gertrude Monro Higgs

UNDERNEATH THE CLOTHES

I'm sure that no one ever knows
The fun I have beneath the clo'es.
I snuggle down inside the bed,
And cover all my face and head.

It's p'raps a coal-mine, p'raps a cave,
And sometimes, when I'm very brave,
It's Daniel's den with three or four
Or even six real lions that roar.

It's most exciting how it goes,
The road that leads beneath the clo'es;
You never can tell how it ends,
Because, you see, it all depends.

Madeleine Nightingale

WHEN FLORA CAME TO TEA

When Flora brought her dolls to tea,
 I did not think her kind.
She said my Dora's head was cracked,
 And had a bump behind.

And Golly, who is *such* a dear,
 She called " a perfect fright! "
I know he's ugly, still, to make
 Remarks is not polite.

For though I think her Beatrice May
 Not *half* so sweet as Dora,
It would be rude to mention it
 When I have tea with Flora.

Catherine A. Morin

THE CHRISTMAS PARTY

We're going to have a party
 And a lovely Christmas tea,
And flags and lighted candles
 Upon the Christmas tree!

And silver balls and lanterns,
 Tied on with golden string,
Will hide among the branches
 By little bells that ring.

74

And then there will be crackers
  And caps and hats and toys,
A Christmas cake and presents
  For all the girls and boys.

With dancing, games and laughter,
  With music, songs and fun,
We'll make our Christmas Party
  A joy for everyone!

Adeline White

Myself

SAFETY FIRST

Up the street I look to see
If any traffic's near to me;
Down the street I look as well,
And listen for a horn or bell.

There's something coming—wait a bit!
If I run out I may be hit!

But now the road is really clear,
No car or motor-bus is near,
I'll run across the road so wide. . .
HURRAH! I'm safe the other side!

Enid Blyton

GOOD RESOLUTIONS

If I were a cobbler,
It should be my pride
The best of all cobblers to be.

If I were a tinker,
No tinker beside
Should mend an old kettle like me.

WHAT MIGHT HAVE BEEN

The little birds are singing
  Above their speckled eggs,
The daddy-long-legs talks about
  His children's lovely legs.

The red cow thinks her little calf
  The best that there can be,
And my papa and my mamma
  Are very proud of me!

And yet I might have been a bird,
  And slept within a nest,
Or been a daddy-long-legs
  With scarcely any chest;

Or been a little calf or pig,
  And grown to beef or ham;
I'm very, very, very glad
  That I am what I am!

Fred E. Weatherly

76

THE OTHER ME

He goes beside me in the sun;
    And he is dark, though I am fair;
Both when I walk, and when I run,
    The Other Me is always there!

I often tell him things I know,
    But not a word has he to say;
Yet still he goes the roads I go,
    And likes to play the games I play.

Sometimes the Other Me is tall,
    And stretches far, far down the street;
Sometimes the Other Me is small,
    And tries to hide beneath my feet!

Last week the Other Me was lost,
    One bad day when it rained and blowed;
He hid when he was wanted most,
    But where he went I never knowed.

He came back when the lamp was lit;
    I saw him dance across the floor,
And jump into my bed, and sit;
    How queer I never heard the door!

Hamish Hendry

COMPARISONS

The elephant is very large,
  And I am very small;
The snail might say as much to me,
  He'd think me very tall!

A rose is to a ladybird
  A palace great and sweet;
As big as houses must appear
  To children in the street.

And stars, that look so wee, are big,
  Some bigger than the sun;
And yet they sprinkle all the sky,
  Like currants in a bun.

And though I'm really seven years old,
  So large, compared with me,
Is Daddy's car—when I get down,
  I feel I'm scarcely three!

Catherine A. Morin

BREAVIN' ON THE WINDOW PANE

It's cold an' grey an' still outside,
And everything is wet with rain.
I'm standing on the cushion seat,
And breavin' on the window pane,
An' drawin' pictures with me 'and.
The window's high against the sky—
I can't see out unless I stand.

I've drawn a house an' chimley pot;
I've drawn a man an' child'en too,
A napple an' a toasting fork,
An' someone who is jus' like you,
An' Granma sittin' in the rain.
The pane's so small I've filled it all,
And 'speks I'll have to breave again.

But Jane has spoilt it now: she says
I want a whippin'—an' I don't.
She's rubbed the window clean, and says
She'll fetch a policeman—*but she won't.*
And now she's gone downstairs again. . .
I'm breavin' on the window pane.
I'll draw a nugly one of Jane.

Marion St. John Webb

79

OF MYSELF AND MY BATH

If instead of socks and vest
In fur and feathers I were drest,
Or scales instead of wool and silk,
I'd keep myself as clean as milk.
For Tabby's small pink tongue will do
For soap and sponge and towel too;
And sparrows when they want a bath
Just wallow in the powdered path;
And fishes do not stay a minute
Out of their bath—they're always in it.

Wilfrid Thorley

MANNERS

It's very rude to cough or sneeze
And not to say, " Excuse me, please."
And nursie says it makes her wild
To see a badly brought-up child.

You mustn't push when in a crowd,
You mustn't talk out very loud,
You mustn't lean against the rails,
You mustn't bite your finger-nails.

You mustn't leave an open door,
You mustn't stamp upon the floor,
And if they question you a lot,
It's very rude to answer, " What ? "

And children (this is quite absurd)
Must all be seen, but never heard.
It surely, surely can't be right,
For you must speak to be polite.

Florence Hoatson

WHEN WE ARE MEN

Jim says a sailor man
   He means to be;
He'll sail a splendid ship
   Out on the sea.

Dick wants to buy a farm
   When he's a man;
He'll get some cows and sheep
   Soon as he can.

Tom says he'll keep a shop;
   Nice things to eat,
Two windows full of cakes,
   Down in the street.

I'd hate a stuffy shop—
   When I'm a man
I'll buy a trotting horse
   And caravan.

E. Stella Meade

TRAINS

Our garden's very near the trains;
    I think it's jolly fine
That I have just to climb the fence
    To watch the railway line!

I love to see the train that takes
    A minute to the mile;
The engine-man, as he goes past,
    Has only time to *smile*!

Then comes a train with empty trucks,
    That never goes so fast;
Its driver-man has always time
    To *wave* as he goes past!

The man who drives the luggage train,
    That passes here at three,
Not only smiles and waves his hand,
    But *whistles* once for me!

Hope Shepherd

THE GOOD LITTLE GIRL

It's funny how often they say to me, " Jane,
Have you been a *good* girl ? "
" Have you been a *good* girl ? "
And when they have said it, they say it again,
" Have you been a *good* girl ? "
" Have you been a *good* girl ? "

I go out to a party, I go out to tea,
I go to an aunt for a week at the sea,
I come back from school or from playing a game;
Wherever I come from, it's always the same: " Well ?
Have you been a *good* girl, Jane ? "

It's always the end of the loveliest day:
" Have you been a *good* girl ? "
" Have you been a *good* girl ? "
I went to the Zoo, and they waited to say:
" Have you been a *good* girl ? "
" Have you been a *good* girl ? "

Well, what did they think that I went there to do ?
And why should I want to be bad at the Zoo ?
And should I be likely to say if I had ?
So that's why it's funny of Mummy and Dad,
This asking and asking, in case I was bad, " Well ?
Have you been a *good* girl, Jane ? "

A. A. Milne

PUPPY AND I

I met a Man as I went walking;
We got talking,
Man and I.
" Where are you going to, Man ? " I said.
   (I said to the Man as he went by.)
" Down to the village, to get some bread.
   Will you come with me ? " " No, not I."

I met a Horse as I went walking;
We got talking,
Horse and I.
" Where are you going to, Horse, today ? "
   (I said to the Horse as he went by.)
" Down to the village to get some hay.
   Will you come with me ? " " No, not I."

I met a Woman as I went walking;
We got talking,
Woman and I.
" Where are you going to, Woman, so early ? "
   (I said to the Woman as she went by.)
" Down to the village to get some barley.
   Will you come with me ? " " No, not I."

I met some Rabbits as I went walking;
We got talking,
Rabbits and I.
" Where are you going in your brown fur coats ? "
   (I said to the Rabbits as they went by.)
" Down to the village to get some oats.
   Will you come with us ? " " No, not I."

I met a Puppy as I went walking;
We got talking,
Puppy and I.
" Where are you going this nice fine day ? "
   (I said to the Puppy as he went by.)
" Up in the hills to roll and play."
   " I'll come with you, Puppy," said I.

A. A. Milne

NEW SHOES

I'm walking on the pavement with my head held high
And my knees held stiff
And my shoes kept dry,
For the streets are awf'ly muddy when the cars splash by,
So I'm walking on the pavement with my head held high.

There's a manly sort of whistle and it comes from me,
And the people think
I'm a man, you see;
And I stump along the pavement just as steady as can be,
There's a manly sort of whistle and it comes from me.

There's a lovely sort of banging when my feet go down,
And my nice new shoes
Are a nice bright brown,
And the pavements kind of echo when I walk in town,
There's a lovely sort of banging when my feet go down.

Caryl Brahms

THE LOOKING-GLASS

Every day Mummy goes down to the shops,
  And sometimes I go as well;
And of all the things we see in town
  I'd never have time to tell.

Today, while Mummy was buying some eggs,
  I waited for her outside,
And there I saw a little green girl
  Whose shoe-lace had come untied.

She stopped to tie it, and so did I;
  I smiled, and she did the same;
Then we both turned away and both peeped back—
  It seemed like playing a game.

She wore a pretty green dress like mine,
  Green stockings up to her knee;
And who do you think was that little green girl?
  Why, that little green girl was ME!

Ruth Underwood

IF NO ONE EVER MARRIES ME

If no one ever marries me—
  And I don't see why they should,
For nurse says I'm not pretty,
  And I'm seldom very good.

If no one ever marries me
  I shan't mind very much,
I shall buy a squirrel in a cage,
  And a little rabbit hutch;

I shall have a cottage near a wood,
  And a pony all my own,
And a little lamb, quite clean and tame,
  That I can take to town.

And when I'm getting really old—
  At twenty-eight or -nine
I shall buy a little orphan-girl
  And bring her up as mine.

Laurence Alma-Tadema

87

THE SECRET

I've got such a wonderful secret,
   Would you like to know it as well?
I told it to Pussy this morning,
   And I am sure Pussy won't tell.

Well, come right away in the corner,
   We mustn't let anyone hear;
Stoop down, and while Nurse isn't looking
   I'll whisper it into your ear.

Last night I peeped into the study—
   But nobody knew I was there—
And I found a magnificent dolly
   In a box on dear Daddy's armchair.

Oh! her hair was so lovely and curly—
   I only gave one little peep—
And her dress was all satin and spangles,
   And her sweet little eyes were asleep.

Now Daddy's too old for a dolly,
   And Baby is only just three;
I'm going to be seven tomorrow,
   And I think that dolly's for *me*.

Jessie Pope

LITTLE THINGS

When God makes a lovely thing,
  The fairest and completest,
He makes it little, don't you know,
  For little things are sweetest.

Little birds and little flowers,
  Little diamonds, little pearls;
But the dearest things on earth
  Are the little boys and girls.

MOTHER

Hundreds of stars in the pretty sky,
  Hundreds of shells on the shore together,
Hundreds of birds that go singing by,
  Hundreds of lambs in the sunny weather.

Hundreds of dewdrops to greet the dawn,
  Hundreds of bees in the purple clover,
Hundreds of butterflies on the lawn,
  But only one mother the whole world over.

George Cooper

CRADLE SONG

What does little birdie say
In her nest at peep of day?
" Let me fly," says little birdie,
" Mother, let me fly away."

" Birdie, rest a little longer,
Till the little wings are stronger."
So she rests a little longer,
Then she flies away.

What does little baby say
In her bed at peep of day?
Baby says, like little birdie,
" Let me rise and fly away."

" Baby, sleep a little longer,
Till the little limbs are stronger.
If she sleeps a little longer,
Baby, too, shall fly away."

Alfred, Lord Tennyson

A CHRISTMAS SONG

Winds through the olive trees
   Softly did blow
Round little Bethlehem
   Long, long ago.

Sheep on the hillsides lay
   White as the snow;
Shepherds were watching them
   Long, long ago.

Then from the happy skies
   Angels bent low,
Singing their songs of joy,
   Long, long ago.

For, in His manger bed,
   Cradled, we know,
Christ came to Bethlehem
   Long, long ago.

A CHILD'S PRAYER

Father, we thank Thee for the night
And for the pleasant morning light,
For rest and food and loving care,
And all that makes the world so fair.

Help us to do the things we should,
To be to others kind and good,
In all we do, in all we say,
To grow more loving every day.

Rebecca J. Weston

Index of First Lines

Acknowledgments

The Compilers and Publishers desire to make grateful acknowledgment to the following for permission to include copyright poems as stated:

Messrs. Appleton-Century-Crofts, Inc. for " The Elf and the Dormouse " by Oliver Herford from *St. Nicholas Magazine* and *Artful Antics*.

Mrs. V. B. Beevor for " The Secret " by Jessie Pope.

Messrs. Blackie & Son, Ltd. for " The Blot " by M. K. Westcott, " When We Are Men " by E. Stella Meade and " Trains " by Hope Shepherd.

Messrs. Basil Blackwell & Mott, Ltd. for " Underneath the Clothes " by Madeleine Nightingale.

Miss Enid Blyton for " Somebody's Always Pleased " and " Safety First."

Miss Caryl Brahms for " New Shoes."

Miss Marchette Chute for " Circus."

The Clarendon Press, Oxford, for " The Rabbits " by Lucy Diamond, " The Tabby Cat " by Agnes G. Herbertson and " The Snowdrops " and " Snowdrop Time " by Annie Matheson.

Miss Mary Daunt for " Ducks."

Messrs. J. M. Dent & Sons, Ltd. for " The Witch " by Percy Ilott from *Songs of English Childhood*.

Messrs. Gerald Duckworth & Co., Ltd. for " The Vulture " from *Cautionary Verses* by Hilaire Belloc.

Messrs. Evans Brothers, Ltd. for " Apple Harvest " by Helen Leuty and " The Christmas Party " by Adeline White from *The Book of a Thousand Poems*.

Miss Eleanor Farjeon for " Mary and Her Kitten," " Little Lambs " and " Uncle."

Miss Eleanor Farjeon and Messrs. Michael Joseph, Ltd. for " Mrs. Peck Pigeon " from *Silver Sand and Snow*.

Messrs. John Farquharson, Ltd. for " Which? " by Edith Nesbit.

Miss Elizabeth Fleming for " Spiders and Flies " and " Pancakes."

Messrs. George G. Harrap & Co., Ltd. for " Dicky-birds " by Natalie Joan from *Lilts for Little People*, " Autumn " by Florence Hoatson from *The Little White Gate*, " Manners " by Florence Hoatson from *Lavender's Blue* and " Breavin' on the Window Pane " by Marion St. John Webb from *The Littlest One: His Book*.

Miss Ruth Hendry for " Mr. Snowman " and " The Other Me " by Hamish Hendry.

The Houghton Mifflin Company for " Daisies " by Frank Dempster Sherman.

Miss Emily Lewis for " My Dog."